CW00781443

365 DAYS OF MIN.
TO DECLUTTER YOUR MIND

Written by: Jamie Stewart

Copyright © 2016

All Rights Reserved

Warning-Disclaimer

Table Of Contents

Introduction

The contemporary world is filled with stresses, distractions, and challenges; an increasing number of people are constantly searching for useful and reliable "tools" that can bring clarity, fulfillment and happiness in their life.

How this book is organized? There are the following parts:

Part I: The basics of mindfulness

This chapter helps you to learn the basics of mindfulness, such as the laws of nature, better understanding of the present moment awareness, living in the present moment, and so on. You will start exploring the beauty of mindful living.

Part II: Mindfulness meditation

In this part, you will be able to pick up tips and ways to get yourself motivated to meditate. You will learn the core of mindfulness meditations, as well as the techniques to reap the benefits of mindfulness in your life.

Part III: 36 things mindful people do differently every day

Part III is all about engaging the right attitudes, as well as practical tips that everyone can apply to their life. We will explain all the benefits of practicing mindfulness in day-to-day life.

Part IV: Mindfulness and an attitude of gratitude

As the name says, in this chapter, we will be able to discover how to use the mindfulness practice of gratitude to improve our well-being.

Part V: Bring mindfulness into your day

This is the most creative part of the book, in which we unlock the treasure chest and find out practical ways to live mindfully and happy. It will give a power boost to your mindfulness and meditation practice.

The Basics of Mindfulness

The founder of Mindfulness-Based Stress Reduction, Jon Kabat-Zinn, said: "Mindfulness is the awareness that arises through paying attention, on purpose, in the present moment, non-judgmentally. It's about knowing what is on your mind."

When it comes to mindfulness meditation, it is an adaptation of traditional Buddhist meditation practices such as Vipassana. As a matter of fact, the term "Mindfulness" is the western translation for the Buddhist term "Anapanasati" – mindfulness of breathing. However, this ancient practice may have profound relevance for our present-day lives. You do not have to become a Buddhist, it is all about waking up and living in peace and harmony with yourself and with the world. It's hard changing your worldview, but understanding the science of mindfulness may change your life and set you free. It doesn't cost anything to try!

The key to mindfulness is an appreciation for the present moment, which is the direct opposite of taking life for granted. Mindfulness is the end of the ego and its illusion; that's the end of suffering. It can sound a bit odd, but happiness can only be found in the present moment, right here and now.

Bring Mindfulness into Your Day

Why practice mindfulness? Thanks to the work of many researchers like Jon Kabat-Zinn and others, we can understand that mindfulness improves our life in so many ways. There are numerous psychological and physical benefits of practicing mindfulness. Many studies have shown that mindfulness practice can improve mood and health (both physical and mental), as well as boost our overall well-being.

Through these researches, we find out that mindfulness is an effective treatment for stress-related diseases such as chronic pain, cancer, etc.

a. Mindfulness can literally change your brain.

Mindfulness is great for our mental health; it reduces negative emotions and stress. These researchers suggest a clear role of mindfulness in fighting depression, anxiety, and other mental disorders. It may be as good as antidepressants.

Neuroscientists have proven that practicing mindfulness affects certain brain functions. It includes our perception, emotion regulation, introspection, complex thinking, and so on. Therefore, it can change the brain structure and potentially improve all areas of your life.

Sara Lazar, a neuroscientist at Massachusetts General Hospital and Harvard Medical School, says, "We found differences in brain volume after eight weeks in five different regions in the brains of the two groups. In the group that learned meditation, we found thickening in four regions:

1. The primary difference, we found in the posterior cingulate, which is involved in mind wandering, and self relevance.

2. The left hippocampus, which assists in learning, cognition, memory and emotional regulation.

3. The temporo parietal junction, or TPJ, which is associated with perspective taking, empathy and compassion.

4. An area of the brain stem called the Pons, where a lot of regulatory neurotransmitters are produced.

The amygdala, the fight or flight part of the brain which is important for anxiety, fear and stress in general. That area got smaller in the group that went through the mindfulness-based stress reduction program. The change in the amygdala was also correlated to a reduction in stress levels."

b. Mindfulness protects and improves your physical health

When it comes to physical health, mindfulness meditation strengthens your immune system naturally. As you probably already know, your immune system does an important job of defending you against diseases.

c. Mindfulness can improve our focus and productivity

Mindfulness or living in the moment is a state of open and deliberate attention on the present moment. It implies openness for yourself, other people, and the surrounding world.

In addition to all these benefits, mindfulness can help prisoners, veterans, health care professionals, schools, parents, children, and others. Mindfulness is a great practice to motivate yourself in the midst of your hectic day. If you are fully present in right now, some great things are going to happen.

Finding Peace to Live in the Moment

There are numerous challenges that will occur on your spiritual path. If you are able to control your mind, it will be free of reactive bad patterns. Accordingly, if you can control your mind, you will be able to control the situation. By maintaining a moment-by-moment awareness, we accept that our lives unfold only in moments; thus, we achieve a greater sense of peace.

Fundamentally, this is a quite simple concept; the main idea is to clear your mind and feel relaxed right here and now. Why is it still difficult for many people? Ultimately, people find it hard to turn it into a habit. Here're a few additional tips you may find useful.

a. Mindfulness involves acceptance; we should pay attention to our thoughts without labeling them as "good" or "bad". Everyone who wants to bring more mindfulness into their life, should stop identifying with their thoughts and giving them any power – that's all.

b. Mindfulness is a presence in the moment. Being mindful of the present moment, including the dreams and fears that you have, can help you find peace and happiness within your life.

c. In order to truly know yourself, you need to be consciously aware of what you have right now and who you are. The concept of mindfulness is about connecting the mind and the body. After all, everything starts with you. Give mindfulness practice a wholehearted try and see it for yourself. Now, it's your move. Good luck!

THE BASICS OF MINDFULNESS

You can live your life to the fullest.

Essentially, personal development is impossible without self-awareness. You need to learn how to become more open. Self-awareness is a kind of introspection and the starting point that leads to self-improvement. By practicing mindfulness on a day-to-day basis, you will start thinking about whatever it is that you are doing. At the same time, you stop thinking about your past or your future.

1. Bring more mindfulness into your life right now.

Everyone has a couple of minutes each day for personal development. Experience the power of mindful living by practicing "meditation minute". Simply set the time for only one minute. Now close your eyes and focus your full attention on your breathing. Don't think about anything else. This is one of the best meditation practices when you are under stress.

2. How to live fully in the present moment?

"When the Sun goes down at sunset, it will take a part of your life with it." – Native American Proverb.

Mindfulness or living in the moment is a state of open and deliberate attention on the present moment. One of the most popular ways to achieve a state of mindfulness is to rearrange your priorities. Every time you wake up, ask yourself, "What good things am I going to do today?"

3. Exercise – what mindfulness means to me?

Take a few minutes and think of word "mindfulness". Then, write down every word that pops into your head. Don't overthink it and just write down what occurs to you right now.

4. Understanding the laws of nature.

Nature is one of our best friends. Nature is a philosopher and guide when we understand its laws.

Here's the simple way to connect with a higher spirit through nature. Just keep your eyes open and start looking around you. That's enough for the beginning.

5. Practice mindful listening.

In the most cases, we are not focusing on listening to the other person; we are preoccupied with the noise in our own heads. How can we listen more effectively? Here are a few tips to become a better listener.

    a.   Meditate on a regular basis.

    b.   Being present.

    c.   Practice relaxation techniques on a daily basis.

    d.   A few times a day, shut out distractions such as electronic devices and music.

    e.   Learn how to empathize with other people and understand their needs.

6. Let go of self-criticism.

You can benefit from the increased awareness that practicing mindfulness can bring. One of the greatest benefits is to remember to be mindful and letting go of your self-criticism. Here is a great idea to help you to silence your inner critic.

Just say, "Who cares? Big deal!" Therefore, it doesn't matter if it's good enough or not. If your inner critic continues to hold you back, you can say one more powerful sentence – "Why not?" The judge inside you will become speechless. Give it a try!

7. The importance of self-awareness.

Essentially, personal development is impossible without self-awareness. You need to learn how to become more open. Self-awareness is a kind of introspection and the starting point that leads to self-improvement. Here is a simple way to increase your self-awareness – stop and listen to your inner voice. When your mind is calm, you can hear your inner wisdom.

Actually, our inner wisdom speaks to us, but we can't hear it because we are distracted by external noise. Thus, calm down and take your time out.

"Everyone who wills can hear their inner voice. It is within everyone." – Mahatma Gandhi.

8. How to listen to your inner wisdom I?

Do not try to push things. Just be. Several times a day, try to clear your mind. Breathe in and out, and imagine your lungs filling up with fresh and wonderful air. Better?

Calm down, ask for guidance, and just listen. Don't put pressure on yourself to get an answer immediately. If you get your answer, it is good. If you do not get the answer it is good as well. The right answer will come at the right time and right place. In the meantime, live right now.

9. How to listen to your inner wisdom II?

This advice is just that simple – Stop trying and enjoy your life. When you're concerned about what might go wrong in your life, when you create imaginary problem, you can't hear your inner voice. Therefore, relax and do not try to figure it all out.

10. How to listen to your inner wisdom III?

Our life is filled with both ups and downs. All you have to do is calm down. And pay attention to the little things. Every moment is a new opportunity. Listen to it more carefully. Every person comes with the message. Listen to what he or she says.

11. How to listen to your inner wisdom IV?

Life is supposed to be fun. Period. When was the last time you really had fun?

Play with your pet. Make simple crafts with your kids. Play Frisbee in the park. Watch comedy movies and eat popcorn. There are numerous activities that can make you happy. We get our best ideas when we are relaxed and happy. Have fun!

12. Embrace your mistakes as life's lessons.

Your mistakes can help you to improve and become a better person. Your mistakes are life's lessons. When you accept full responsibility for your life, you will see your mistakes as an opportunity to learn and grow.

13. Do not force results.

You are constantly seeking ideas to improve your mindfulness and become a better person. That's great!

However, it seems like you don't have "significant" results. It feels like everyone else is doing better than you. Thus, you can get frustrated. Wait a second. Follow this simple rule – don't force results. Just keep up the good work. And wait for God's timing to make it happen.

14. Stop comparing yourself to others.

Did you know that comparison with others tends to lower your self-esteem? To be happy and content, you have to go your own way.

15. Practicing mindfulness in everyday life.

How to make mindfulness a practical reality in your life? Pay attention to whatever's going on right now, whether it's an internal or external experience. Try to notice the world around you. And keep a sharp mind and a good attitude.

16. Am I on the right path?

Here are three important questions to ask yourself.

    a.   Am I happy with my life?

    b.   Do I wake up feeling excited about a new day?

    c.   Am I helping the world to be a better place?

Basically, the first answer that pops into your mind will be your truth. Further, it would be good if you can think of these questions and answer them through your meditation.

17. Activities to make you happier.

a. Appreciate a wonderful sunny day.

b. Donate money, clothes, money, or other belongings.

c. Volunteer your time. This is a great way to help others, be useful, and feel that we are serving someone beyond ourselves.

d. Take a nap a few times a day.

18. A few tips to feel more grateful.

You may be feeling a bit like a failure, but you are definitely not. You have the power to choose. Instead of complaining about your life, choose to be grateful for it.

a. Learn to live in the moment. Focus your full attention on your breathing several times per day.

b. Appreciate what you already have. If you are contented with what you have, not with what you lack, you create an abundance mentality.

c. Watch your thoughts. Your thoughts become your habits and your actions. Thinking about all we have to appreciate will boost our happiness.

19. The present moment is free of suffering.

When we live in our future or past, we miss out on the peace in the present moment. When you are "living" in the past or future, you feel resentment, anger, envy, lack, mistrusting and other negative emotions. And you are suffering.

How do we find happiness? Where do we look? The present moment is all you have. Mindfulness is the end of the ego and its illusion. And that's the end of suffering. Happiness can only be found in the present moment, right here and right now.

20. You are not your thoughts.

If you want to bring more mindfulness into your life, stop identifying with your thoughts. Did you notice that thoughts come and go, but they are never the real you? Why? That's because your thoughts are not aware of you, but being aware of your thoughts can help you bring more mindfulness into your life. Stop giving your thoughts power and that's it! Easy.

21. A great way to stay present in the moment – write a journal.

Many distractions keep you from connecting with yourself and other people. It can lead to depression, anxiety, stress, and physical illness.

Write a journal almost every day; it can help you stay present in the moment and spark new ideas. If you regularly record your thoughts, you will have insight into your moods and personal growth. Writing your thoughts every day may help to open up your unconscious mind. In addition, keeping a journal can help you in the healing process.

How to get started? Here are some guidelines, but try to write it in your own words, following your heart.

a. Ask yourself: Where you are in your life, at this moment?

b. Just follow your "stream of consciousness."

c. Here's a great way to develop your intuition. Write down your question; take a deep breath and be open to listen for a response.

d. Make a gratitude list.

22. The art of now.

We need to live in the present moment. When we become mindful, we suddenly realize that we are not our thoughts.

Don't try so hard to control your thoughts. Instead of that, just accept your thoughts, observe them, and come into the present. That's it. Remember – you are not your thoughts.

23. Just stay open to receive.

Mindfulness requires no belief and no religion. Remember – mindfulness is for all, and this is scientifically based. From now onward, you will be able to develop your wellbeing with proven techniques that mindfulness offers to you. Forget all religious dogma and ask yourself – what mindfulness means to me? You can receive your answer thorough the meditation. Sometimes, we get our best ideas when we least expect it (e.g. when we take a shower). Just stay open to receive.

24. The process of being mindful requires your intention.

Your intention will reduce your stress and develop wisdom. Being sure about what you hope to get from mindfulness shapes the quality of your spiritual experience. Otherwise, if you are not sure about your intentions and goals, there's a good chance that it will get you nowhere. You are just like a ship without a sail.

25. A state of being aware of something.

If you tend to develop a wide and open awareness, you should focus your attention on something. For instance, you can focus your attention on a part of your body and breathe.

Then, while meditating you can choose to focus on a particular object. Therefore, intentionally paying attention to your present moment, you practice your mindfulness.

26. Mindful breathing really works.

The best place to start to experience being mindful is with your breath. Stop whatever you are doing. Then, take five to ten mindful breaths. It will take no more than about 20 seconds. This simple exercise will improve your concentration as well.

27. Hold on for a brighter future.

"Realize deeply that the present moment is all you ever have. Make the Now the primary focus of your life." – Eckhart Tolle

The only moment that exists is the present moment. When we honor the present moment, it ironically leads to a brighter future!

28. An exercise for the present moment awareness.

If you are fully present in right now, some great things are going to happen. However, you have to motivate yourself in the midst of your hectic day. Here's a practical exercise to help you live in the present moment. When you wash your hands, be aware of the water (e.g. Is the water cold or warm?); now, smell the soap, touch it gently and feel its textures. Do the simple thing and gradually retrain your mind.

"Drink your tea slowly and reverently, as if it is the axis on which the world earth revolves – slowly, evenly, without rushing toward the future; live the actual moment. Only this moment is life." – Thich Nhat Hanh

29. How can I add greater value to the world?

If you think that you have to create something that will blow someone's mind, it is not true. For instance, smile at someone and be kind. For example: Smile anytime you begin a conversation. Your new habit will make the world a better place. It really is as simple as that.

"Making one person smile can change the world; maybe not the whole world, but their world." – Pravinee Hurbungs

30. Thoughts become reality.

Your inner dialogue is constantly going on in your mind. During your day, what do you think about? Do you think about your strengths? Or your weaknesses? Are you concerned about your future?

Our thoughts are creative. If you worry, you will create more worries and negative thoughts. If you have happy thoughts, you attract more and more happy thoughts. Once you realize the power of thoughts, that's the point of no return. Watch your thoughts.

31. You are the creator of your life.

Do you think that you are at the mercy of external events? Actually, the truth is that your life is a result of the choices you made and the thoughts you have chosen to think. Norman Vincent Peale said, "Change your thoughts and you change your world."

It isn't just that simple. You can transform your reality by practicing techniques of mindfulness. It requires some time and patience. However, it's worth it because your happiness has no price.

32. Getting started with mindfulness in an easy way.

Kindness to yourself is a very important aspect of mindfulness. When practicing mindfulness, you should be kind to yourself. If you have an inner critic, let the judgement go. Mindfulness encourages you to be aware of the self-criticism.

33. How to quiet self-criticism?

Every day, our inner dialogue sounds like this: What's wrong with me? I can't do anything right. I'm ugly. And so on. We often think that self-judgment can ensure we achieve our goals. It drains our energy and confidence and paralyzes progress. Here's what actually happens to you – You become your own worst enemy!

If you want to change how you speak to yourself, here's a great idea. Observe your thoughts, without judging them or taking them seriously. For example, "I am ugly," becomes "I'm having the thought that I am ugly." Observe your self-critical thoughts from day to day. Over time it just becomes easier and one day you will achieve constructive self-criticism.

34. How to practice self-compassion?

Practice self-compassion and explore your thoughts through writing. Answer the question: Why you feel shame and what causes it? Take a few minutes to think.

Step 1: Write down your answers by making a list.

Step 2: Don't fight that feeling, observe your shame and accept it as an active process of acknowledging your present-moment.

Step 3: Take responsibility for your feeling of shame. What's done is done, it's time to let go.

Step 4: Let it go and decide to move towards your goals no matter what.

35. How to explore self-compassion?

Here's a great exercise.

Write a letter to yourself from the perspective of your imaginary friend. Imagine that he or she loves you unconditionally. Your friend knows your life history and he can see all your strengths and weaknesses. What would he or she write to remind you that all people have both strengths and weaknesses? Try to write with kindness and caring. Put your letter down and come back tomorrow in order to read it again.

36. Incorporate it into a daily practice.

If you want to develop a consistent mindful way of living, a daily practice is a must. Without a daily routine and the practice of staying present, you may struggle to be mindful in everyday situations.

"Practice is everything. This is often misquoted as Practice makes perfect." – Periander.

37. How to be here and now?

Our present moment experiences can be internal (e. g. thoughts or emotions) or external (whatever we perceive using our senses). In order to be here, you should focus on something. For instance, the sensations that are happening inside your body at this moment.

38. One of the best practices for being present – openness.

Mindfulness encourages you to open up to your inner and outer experiences. This is a sense of stepping back from your emotions and experiences. You don't run away from them; you just observe them without the need to attach to them. In this way, you can easily deal with your emotions.

39. Using mindfulness to change habits.

William James, the famous philosopher, wrote 125 years ago:

"Any sequence of mental action which has been frequently repeated tends to perpetuate itself; so that we find ourselves automatically prompted to think, feel, or do what we have been before accustomed to think, feel, or do, under like circumstances, without any consciously formed purpose, or anticipation of results. "(James 1890, 112)

Honestly, almost all of us have habits that we would like to change. To change your unhealthy habits, you need to create new patterns – new neural pathways in your brain. Ask yourself: At what times am I on autopilot? The answer will help you reflect on the activities of your life in which you're not fully present. Maybe, these activities have negative consequences for you.

40. Identifying bad habits.

Mindfulness can give you an opportunity to transform your behaviors. Here is an exercise that can help you identify your bad habits. These are the actions and thoughts that don't serve your well-being.

Take some time to write down your response to the following question without judging yourself: Do your thoughts and actions have negative consequences for your overall well-being?

41. The key to breaking harmful patterns.

Since our habits develop through repetition, it's enough to recognize our unhealthy patterns. All you have to do is to create new patterns. Mindfulness is the key component to healing from the stresses of being caught up in bad patterns and unhealthy habits. Then, compassion and kindness toward yourself are the most important emotions here.

Write down your answer to this question: Does your habit separate you from yourself or your friends and family? You will get a closer insight into your bad habit.

42. Mindfulness as your morning routine.

For example, try to brush your teeth consciously. When you brush your teeth, notice the sounds and smell, feel the water and the movements of your arms.

Basically, you should focus on the things that you can feel, smell or hear (feel physically) at the moment. You can also use other morning activities such as shaving, brushing your hair or having a shower.

43. Seeing the world with a fresh perspective.

This is a quick and easy exercise to connect with your environment. Pick some domestic chores such as washing dishes or vacuuming floors, and do it consciously.

Mindfulness is about developing and improving an awareness of your present moment experiences and a greater sense of wellbeing.

44. Mindfulness exercise – notice three things.

Throughout the day, pause for a moment and look around. Notice three things you can see around. Then, listen carefully, and notice three things you can hear. You can record your experiences in your notebook.

45. A simple tip for a mindful life.

Here's an easy exercise to center yourself and live more mindful life.

For example, when some feeling arises, simply note "feelings". Say the word "feelings" in your mind. Then, note your feeling by name such as "shame" or "boredom".

46. A childlike curiosity.

The simplest approaches can often lead to the deepest insights.

Note "words" you can hear in your mind. You should simply observe these words with childlike curiosity, without judging them as good or bad.

47. Practice mindful eating.

Here's an idea to gain a greater sense of meaning in your life. You can practice mindful eating.

Step 1: Response to the following question: Am I hungry?

Step 2: If you are really hungry, ask yourself: What do I eat?

Step 3: Sit down at a table; enjoy your meal without engaging in any other activities. Turn off TV, computer, music, cell phone, etc.

Step 4: Next, eat your food paying full attention to it; chose a piece of food and notice how it looks and how it smells. Chew it slowly and enjoy your eating as a pleasurable activity for satisfying hunger and making you feel full of energy.

48. Practice mindful walking.

A main idea of mindfulness is to help you to stop striving to reach your goal.

Try to concentrate on your breathing and the feel of the ground under your feet while walking. Simply observe what is around you, staying in the now. Then, feel the temperature, rain or sun on your skin.

49. What is going on with me at the moment?

How to make mindfulness a practical reality in your life? Theory is great, but when you experience the benefits of mindfulness in your everyday life, things will never be the same.

Throughout the day, pause for a moment and respond to this simple question: "What is going on with me at the moment?" Notice your emotions and write it down if necessary.

50. Clarifying your purpose.

Consider your expectations from your spiritual journey. Do you want an instant pick-me-up at any time of day? Or improve your relationships? Overcoming challenges? You should align yourself with your goals and clarify your purpose.

51. How to improve your relationships with mindfulness?

According to the definition: "Mindfulness is the act of being consciously aware with mindful attitudes."

a) It means that you can understand your partner's needs.

b) Being mindful of the current moment can reduce stress in your life. Thus, your relationship must be better.

c) You will appreciate the present moment and enjoy spending time with your partner.

52. Mindfulness keeps your brain healthy.

When we can make a distinction between our experience and our interpretations, we can break the cycles of automatic reactivity and rigid beliefs.

"It seems Zen practitioners were able to remove or lessen the averseness of the stimulation – and thus the stressing nature of it – by altering the connectivity between two brain regions which are normally communicating with one another. They certainly don't seem to have blocked the experience. Rather, it seems they refrained from engaging in thought processes that make it painful." – Joshua Grant, a postdoc at the Max Plank Institute for Human Cognitive and Brain Sciences in Leipzig, Germany.

53. Mindfulness and your intellect.

Being mindful of the current moment integrates your emotions with your intellect.

The practice of mindfulness can activate the connections between your intellectual part of the brain and your emotional part of the brain. Thus, you will be able to deal with your emotions in an easy and effective way. For instance, you start to feel when you get angry. Instead of emotionally reacting, you can say: "That's good, this is just a feeling that's arising."

54. How to practice mindful observation?

Pick an object from within your environment. Now focus on watching it for a few minutes. It is a great idea to observe the clouds.

Don't do anything else and try to relax as much as possible. Look at this object like a child, as if you are seeing it for the first time. Think of its purpose in our world.

55. Practice mindful awareness – cooking.

Cooking is a great opportunity to practice mindfulness. Simply feel the food in your hands. Stop and appreciate how lucky you are to have this food to cook and eat with your family. Make even a simple meal as a work of creation. Enjoy!

56. How to practice purposeful awareness?

Throughout the day, take some moments to cultivate purposeful mindfulness. There are many little things that you can do with mindful awareness. Conversation is a great opportunity to practice purposeful awareness. Here is a simple idea you can implement in your daily conversations – Think before you speak.

57. Have a mindful conversation.

Here are a few easy steps to achieve mindful conversation.

Step 1: Turn off all devices such as TV, phone, or computer.

Step 2: Look the other person in the eyes.

Step 3: Learn to stop your mind from wandering. You can achieve that by practicing meditation.

58. How to boost your brainpower?

Exercising for 20 to 30 minutes a day can increase awareness and self-knowledge, as well as boost our brainpower.

Exercise gives us the ability to focus and improve productivity. Everyone can benefit from the physical exercises.

59. Plan your day.

How many days are you designing? Consider planning each and every day. Yes, even Sundays. It is important to challenge yourself on a daily basis.

"If you don't know where you are going, you'll end up someplace else." – Attributed to Yogi Berra

60. Mindful immersion.

Choose a simple everyday task such as doing your laundry Then, pay attention to every detail of that activity, using your mindful attitudes. You will experience your regular routine like never before.

61. Listen to your inner child.

The solution is simple – Don't take things too seriously. Stop and listen to your inner child! Maybe you will hear: "I'd like some ice cream." It's great, let's go get some ice cream.

There's nothing new for you to learn. Mindfulness is the rediscovery of a world you used to live in your childhood.

62. Stop feeling pressured.

Do you feel pressured by time, money or something else?

You just need a slower-paced life. Yes, it is possible to never hurry, but to be successful and get everything done.

Don't rush yourself and stop feeling pressured. "Nature does not hurry, yet everything is accomplished." – Lao Tzu.

Take a few belly breaths. Every time you take a deep breath, you release pressure. Every time you take a deep conscious breath, that's mindfulness.

63. You can live your life to the fullest.

The idea of being more conscious and being present seems impossible to many of us. We can achieve success, but we have trouble living life to the fullest. Here's a practical idea for the super busy people – Do only one thing at a time. Only one thing. There is a famous Zen saying: "When walking, walk. When eating, eat."

64. One-month challenge.

"One-month challenge" is a great exercise for super busy people. Create a monthly schedule. Throughout this month, practice mindful awareness by making little pauses.

If you have a lot of things that must get done, don't schedule them close together. Take a break between each task and practice your mindfulness.

65. Forget about perfectionism.

Perfectionism can really weigh you down. You can't enjoy the moment, you can't relax and live your life to the fullest.

Don't put unnecessary pressure on yourself and allow yourself to make mistakes. There is a proverb: "No one is perfect – that's why pencils have erasers."

66. Mindfulness and changing the brain.

Basically, the more we repeat some thoughts, the more likely we are to keep repeating them. Why? Because it is easier to think thought that you have before. Even when those thoughts hurt.

The Buddha said, "Whatever a bhikkhu (monk, or practitioner) frequently thinks and ponders upon, that will become the inclination of his mind" (Bodhi 1995, 208).

If you think negative thoughts, you train your mind in that direction. However, every time you make a mindful choice and think the motivational and kind thoughts, you will reprogram your brain, little by little. Actually, you reap what you sow.

67. What mindfulness involves?

As we said before, the key component of mindfulness is to be open to every experience just as it is. Why is it so difficult to achieve? Because there're many things that pull us away from the present moment experience. There are too many emotions, sensations, and thoughts.

Being mindful is not easy and it takes time and practice. Try to be aware of moment-to-moment experience and over time, your life will be better.

68. What does mindfulness mean to YOU?

We are all different. The concept of mindfulness may help people in different ways. Ultimately, each of us has different life history and different lives. Therefore, stop comparing with other people. Response to the following questions: What does mindfulness mean to YOU? What YOU want from a mindful life? Write it down.

69. Think less, do more.

It seems contradictory, but when we think less, we can do more. In this way, we can do things more slowly and with more concentration. Therefore, we can use our mindfulness in order to alleviate stress and anxiety as well as boost our productivity.

70. Learn to "Ride the waves".

There is the proverb: If you can't calm the waters learn to ride the waves

Mindfulness will help you learn to be open to different experiences, pleasant and unpleasant, without getting pulled into unwanted behaviors.

71. Take your time.

Don't fill your day with too many tasks. You will be too busy to stop and think about what you do. Instead, you should complete every action slowly and deliberately.

Make your everyday tasks deliberate, not rushed. It takes practice, but when you take your time you focus on the action.

72. Focus on the process.

Concentrate on the process, not on the end result. Cultivate this great skill. It will be useful when you have challenging experiences. This is a great way to release unnecessary pressure from your day and develop beneficial states of mind.

"Success is a journey, not a destination. The doing is often more important than the outcome." –Arthur Ashe

73. Every day is a new beginning.

Mindfulness is not a magic formula. It can't immediately transform our long-established habits. If you have some problem or addiction, it will take time.

You will improve your mindfulness by living mindfully on a day-to-day basis.

74. A prerequisite for true mindfulness – set your intention.

Identify your behaviors that prevent you from living your best life and your purpose. You can find it by asking yourself: "Do my intentions support my deepest aspirations?

Once you have decided what it is you want, align your dreams and desires with your intentions.

75. Write down your intentions.

What matters most to me in life? Write down your highest intentions. Make sure to read it regularly.

Use everyday activities as reminders throughout a day; pause and think what matters most to you.

76. Become comfortable with the silence.

Silence is a beautiful thing. Only five minutes of silence can do wonders for you and your mind. Silence helps you to focus on well-being. Turn off the noise in and around your head. Sit with awareness of thoughts. And don't forget about mindful breathing. Lovely!

77. What action serves my deepest intention?

Imagine this situation. You are relaxing after work. What is the best you could do for yourself? Spend some time with family or drink a glass of wine. Go to the gym or watch your favorite TV show.

If you are unsure, response to the following question: "What action serves my deepest intention?"

78. Your mindset keeps you from true happiness.

Through your day, notice whenever a certain person or situation triggers you to behave or think in a way that is not in alignment with your intentions.

When you have to make a decision, do you get caught up in "negative" thoughts such as fearful, anxious, or judgmental thoughts?

Try to describe emotions and beliefs that are linked to these thoughts. Do you recognize certain patterns that are keeping you from happiness?

79. Your new morning routine.

Take a morning to practice mindfulness and connect with yourself. Bring more awareness into your morning routine by asking yourself: "What is the most important at this moment? My job, my money or my family?" Mindfulness in the morning will prepare you for challenging moments through the day.

80. Cultivating a new shopping habits.

Step 1: To avoid buying on impulse, make a shopping list; put only healthy foods and drinks on the list.

Step 2: Buy only what's on the list. It will help you achieve your goals such as loosing wait or eating healthier. By living mindfully, you become aware of unwanted messages such as advertisements and you stop buying unnecessary things. Good luck!

81. Mindfulness activities.

Time is a real treasure. We spend at least 30 minutes waiting in lines or sitting in traffic, right? You can utilize your time effectively and wisely. You can meditate or breathe mindfully while you wait.

"When you drive around the city and come to a red light or a stop sign, you can just sit back and make use of these twenty or thirty seconds to relax — to breathe in, breathe out, and enjoy arriving in the present moment. There are many things like that we can do." – Thich Nhat Hanh

82. Speak your truth.

If you want to be happy, you have to speak your truth. Being honest takes courage, but it is the path to mindfulness. Speak your truth and clearly help people understand your attitudes.

Additionally, you should listen to others because they have their truths that may be completely different from yours. If you wish to have better relationships, you have to speak mindfully.

83. How to stop overthinking everything.

If you used to overthink each and every little problem, you can't cultivate mindful attitudes. And you get caught up in anxious and judgmental thoughts. You can't notice the world around you. How to stop overthinking?

a. Breathe more and talk less about your worries.

b. Try to get busy as much as possible.

c. Last but not least, practice mindfulness every day. Just live in the present moment.

84. Say goodbye to depression and anxious.

"If you are depressed, you are living in the past, if you are anxious you are living in the future, and if you are at peace you are living in the present." – Lao Tzu.

The present moment is full of opportunities. Make a promise to yourself that you will notice the good things that happens every day. This exercise will help you live more peacefully day-to-day.

85. Bring more playfulness into your world.

Life is fun, we should enjoy every second! Mindfulness can help you to see the world with a fresh perspective. It will also help you to gain a greater sense of wellbeing. As you go throughout the day, stop and ask yourself: How can I make my life more playful?

"We don't stop playing because we grow old; we grow old because we stop playing." – George Bernard Shaw.

86. Take a walk without any plans.

Here's the simple way to connect with a higher spirit through everyday activities. Wear loose and comfortable clothing and take a walk. In addition to physical activity, you will get an instant pick-me-up. And don't forget about mindful breathing all the time.

87. Erase painful memories.

Most of us are still living the emotional pain from our traumatic and painful memories on a daily basis. We are prisoners to our past experiences. It is time to let it go. What has happened cannot be changed.

The solution for this situation may be hiding in the present moment and mindfulness. By living mindfully on a day-to-day basis, you should be able to understand your past and create new memories that will make you smile.

88. A wider perspective.

When you're not at the present moment, you're on autopilot. Exploring the journey of mindful living, you can understand big-picture thinking. Your mindful attitudes give you a wider perspective. Things are not always black or white. Now you become more open to possibilities and you see the world differently.

89. Discover the true YOU.

The spiritual masters claim that the main purpose of human life is to discover the true self. It is called Atman. To achieve that, we should make our vision crystal clear. Mindfulness and self-knowledge can help us to discover our true nature. When you are present in the moment, excluding all external influences, you find out more about yourself. It is a "remedy" for all human problems.

90. Mindfulness is our natural state.

If you have been regularly practicing mindfulness for the past several years and you can't experience peace of mind, don't worry. Mindfulness isn't a forced concentration of mind. There is no need to put in the effort to achieve mental concentration while practicing mindfulness. Mindfulness is our natural state. You already know how doing it; you just need a bit more practice to remind yourself.

91. Changing yourself, changing the world.

"Peace in oneself, peace in the world." – Thich Nhat Hanh.

If you think that you were not born for greater things, think of it this way: What is something you care about that is greater than yourself? Maybe you can make some impact on someone's life. You may realize that you are not powerless. Just give a mindfulness practice a try for a few months!

92. How to build a healthy lifestyle?

What is missing in our normal day to day life?

As we said before, the main purpose of mindfulness is to calm your mind and bring stillness to it. Human brain thinks about everything we do through the day. Your brain calculates your every move. Mindfulness allows us to slow down our frantic mind. This is the key to healthy living. Good health isn't just about healthy eating and physical exercise – it also includes having mindful attitudes and an awareness of the present moment.

93. Mindfulness improves sleep.

By practicing mindfulness, your mind will slow down. In that way, it becomes easier to evoke the relaxation response at night. At the very beginning, just don't worry about how you're doing. Over time, you will improve.

A higher level of mindfulness involves slowing all thoughts so you will be able to fight insomnia. Here are two simple steps you can try to improve your sleep.

    a.   Focus on your breath or a short prayer.

    b.   When you notice your mind starts to wander, gently return your attention to your focus.

94. Mindfulness and thought control.

If you want to control your thoughts by practicing mindfulness, keep in mind that your thoughts are constantly going.

Do not try to eliminate your thoughts and force this process. When you try to control your thoughts they start wandering and you are wasting your time and energy. It can lead to a great deal of frustration.

Thoughts come and go and that's it. Instead of trying to control them, you should cultivate awareness of your thought and develop the skill of observing them.

95. Find your life's passion.

By practicing mindfulness on a day-to-day basis, you will start thinking about whatever it is that you are doing. At the same time, you stop thinking about your past or your future.

You become lost in your work when you love what you are doing. It is called "being in the zone" Artist and sportsmen can focus on the present moment and forget about everything else.

Find your life's passion and practice mindfulness, which will result in a more fulfilling life.

96. Decide to stick with it.

There is a proverb, "Most people are about as happy as they decide to be".

Make a decision to be happy today. Make a strong decision to practice mindfulness every day. Simply like that. It is important to be determined from the start and remember to not give up even if you can't see any results. If you truly want to receive the benefits of mindfulness it takes time.

Keep this tip in your back pocket and remind yourself every time you think to give up.

97. Visualize your results.

You can visualize the benefits you'll receive from mindfulness. Imagine your body cleansing itself of all toxins with each your breath. Visualization of positive results will improve your chances of sticking with practice until you start receiving results.

As long as you keep these benefits in mind, you'll be able to stick to your everyday practice.

98. Decrease negative stimulants.

Avoid negative stimulants such as tobacco and alcohol. Avoid excessive information as a stimulant. When it comes to TV, moderation is the key, for both adults and children. It will improve your chances of enjoying the results of mindfulness living.

99. Choose a time for your practice.

At the very beginning, try to choose a fixed time for your practice. Any exercise you choose, stick to the chosen time. The best time is early morning, but you can choose whatever suits your routine.

100. Choose a place for your practice.

It would be great if you could choose a certain place for your mindful exercises. It would help in sticking to the habit. There is no need to build a special space for it, one little corner of your bedroom can be perfect.

101. How to practice mindful appreciation?

In this exercise, you should notice ten things to be grateful for in your day. Here is the example:

1) Your friends,

2) Family,

3) Health,

4) Sense of sight,

5) Sense of taste,

6) Your immune system,

7) Your mind,

8) Your speech,

9) Happiness,

10) Oxygen.

Make your own list.

102. Close your eyes to see.

A few times a day, close your eyes and breathe. In this way, you will slowly turn your attention inwards. Feel the weight lift off of your chest and observe how you feel about that. You will be able to see things from another perspective. Sometimes, we need to close our eyes in order to see our true path.

103. Discover your true values.

Working on personal growth will bring you higher levels of awareness. In that way, you will be able to discover your true values. There are two questions that can help you find your path.

1) What do you want your legacy to be?

2) If money was no object, how would you spend your time?

Discover your true values and you will find more mindfulness in your life

104. Understanding the importance of self-compassion.

Here's an interesting exercise you can use any time of the day.

Think of a hard situation in your life. Call this situation (event or person) to mind, and observe your feelings. Now you can say: "I am suffering." This is present moment awareness.

Then, you can respond to the following question: "May I give myself the compassion that I need, and accept myself as I am?" You will get an answer soon.

105. How to sit during mindfulness meditation?

a.   First and foremost, sit with a relatively balanced straight back.

b.   Find a comfortable chair and tilt it slightly forwards.

c.   Then, you can place your hands wherever it feels comfortable for you.

d.   Your head should balance on your neck.

e.   Then, find a central balanced place for your body.

106. Forget the past.

"The past is only a tail

You keep dragging behind you

Collecting dust and dirt

Until it's so heavy with bitterness and regret

It stops you moving forward." – Steve Taylor.

Being in the now with your mindfulness means being aware of what is going on right here and now. Here is a practical exercise.

Step 1: Take a deep breath and allow yourself to completely relax.

Step 2: Ask yourself: What is my biggest regret? If I could go back, what would I change?

107. Practice self-observation.

When you practice self-observation from day to day, you automatically change your life. Any time you watch your emotions and thoughts, you are being mindfully aware. As we said before, you are not your thoughts, and you are not your emotions. You are an observer.

108. The transformative power of mindful living.

The world gets busier day by day. Humans experience stress and they need the feeling of freedom for a while.

Mindfulness can help you to improve your balance and move forward in your life.

Developing your practice is like planting a garden. It takes time and patience to feel the transformative power of mindful living. It brings you into contact with your inner being and it is worth the time.

109. We have powerful minds.

The human mind is wonderful, but it can bring us many complications. In fact, we create these complications and troubles. "Life is really simple, but we insist on making it complicated." – Confucius

When we cultivate purposeful mindfulness and if we persist, we will succeed. And don't forget about mindful breathing. We will realize that life is too short to be complicated.

110. Think like a child.

Observe children; they look at things differently. They live simply, without the baggage of all those years, without judgment and concerns for the future. A few times a day, at least once, when you are able, try to think and act like a child. You will be present in the moment, which helps in getting rid of stress.

111. We touch other people's lives.

As we said before, mindful living means bringing awareness to each moment in your life. Mindfulness of thinking and acting changes your life. It also changes the lives of the people around you. Whether we like it or not, we touch other people's lives. Please be aware of that.

112. Mindful actions – Let's do it!

Start each and every day with mindful breathing and mindful attitudes. Every morning, without exception ask yourself: "What is my daily plan? What steps will I take today?" This might be a small action, it doesn't matter. To get things done, you need to take action. Let's do it!

113. A practical exercise.

If you have children, you can take a morning to practice mindful listening and connecting with them before rushing to work. In this way, you can achieve a new state of consciousness. Also, you will know that there are a lot of perspectives through which you can be conscious of the present moment.

114. Prevention of unnecessary impulses.

How about emotional hunger? For instance, you can feel hungry even after you just ate your lunch. You can use mindfulness to get rid of different unnecessary impulse that can occur. Mindfulness meditation provides great results in these situations. This is a great method for people who are suffering from eating disorders and some addictions.

115. The power of appreciation.

To feel appreciation, we have to first be in the present moment. When we live in the moment, we are able to experience appreciation anywhere and anytime.

When you practice mindfulness, you may find that there are quite a lot of things you can easily be appreciative of. Maybe, you become grateful for many things, things that you haven't noticed before.

116. Do not focus too much.

It is the basic rule of mindfulness techniques – too much focus on one thing can make a problem. Actually, mindfulness is about being aware of our whole surroundings. Your mind should go from one thing to another. Of course, you should use your senses to explore things around you. Try to experience each and every thing that your mind can comprehend.

117. Improve your listening comprehension skills.

Here's a great exercise to improve mindful listening. Shut off all other senses and use only your ears to experience the sounds around you. If there are too much noise and distractions, you can focus on ticking sounds that the clock near you makes. Block all other sounds and listen to that ticking sound in order to improve your sense of hearing.

118. Feel your body parts.

Here's another exercise. Try to feel your body parts. Pay attention to each part, one at a time. Feel your feet, then your knees and continue to feel all the body parts, including internal organs. This exercise will help you feel relaxed as well.

119. Try your senses.

Practicing mindfulness is the key to recognizing your inner wisdom.

An effective method for practicing mindfulness is to focus on external sensations. For instance, you can feel the summer heat on your skin. There are so many ways to practice mindfulness in your everyday activities. Be creative and let your imagination run wild!

120. A higher level of self-esteem.

Mindfulness meditation can have a positive effect on one's self-esteem. It can have a big impact on your way of thinking. Your freedom is worth the effort! Try to do some of these exercises (breathing, focus, meditation, etc.) in order to boost yourself before doing something your fear about.

MINDFULNESS MEDITATION

Mindfulness meditation is a lifestyle choice.

Meditation is our natural state of being. After regular practice of mindfulness meditation, we start to know ourselves better. A meditator becomes connected with his/ her true self. This implies knowing yourself as both a physical and spiritual being, in touch with everything that is and the whole creation

121. Mindfulness meditation should help you to stay in the present.

"Meditation is the discovery that the point of life is always arrived at in the immediate moment." – Alan Watts

Mindfulness meditation can help you become aware of the present moment with whatever is happening. If you want to fully participate in your life, practice mindfulness meditation. There are many types of mindfulness meditation such as open awareness meditation, mindfulness of sounds meditation, the body scan meditation, and so on.

122. Preparing for meditation.

Whether you are a very beginner or not, you should prepare for your meditation practice. You should prepare physically and mentally. This is one of the most important steps in learning to meditate. First and foremost, find a quiet location. Then, it is important to create a relaxing atmosphere. Light a candle and breathe; take 8 to 10 slow deep breaths that completely fill your lungs. You are ready.

123. How to do mindful meditation?

a. Find a quiet spot in your home and choose comfortable clothing.

b. Take good posture (half lotus, full lotus, seiza position, on a chair, or lay down)

c. Then, try to feel your breath to settle your mind. Bring your awareness to your breath, while observing it.

d. Remind yourself that you are not your thoughts. Don't follow your thoughts; observe them and just let it go.

e. Make sure to focus only on the present moment and try to focus on the sensations. Don't focus too much, try to relax as much as possible.

124. Relaxation is the key to mindfulness meditation.

One of the most important steps in learning to do mindfulness meditation is that you need to be comfortable. Once you get comfortable, you'll eventually be able to meditate anywhere. It will help you to relax and meditate without hassle.

125. A practical advice.

There's an old proverb: "To be prepared is half the victory". Whether you are a very beginner or not, you should prepare for your mindfulness meditation in a proper way. Here is a great advice – it is good to shower or bathe before you meditate.

126. Physical exercise and meditation go hand in hand.

Do you want a deeper experience of meditation? When you're first starting out learning how to meditate, it is really important to have practical tips and tricks. Don't underestimate the value of physical activities in your life. Physical exercises affect your whole nervous system.

When you exercise, you boost your metabolism and stimulate the flow of nutrients and blood throughout your body. Regular physical activity reduces stress and relieves tension as well. It improves your quality of life. Therefore, physical exercise and meditation go hand in hand. Keep this tip in your back pocket!

127. Posture is really important.

How you sit in meditation is an important factor in your successful practice. A good posture throughout the meditative process allows your body to function at its optimal level. Regardless of whether you choose to sit or stand, focus on keeping your back straight and chest open. A good posture will help you connect the mind and body.

128. Enter into a meditative state faster.

As a matter of fact, there are no rigid rules. You just have to follow your heart. Mindfulness meditation is about calming the mind, right? However, there are a couple of practical advices that can help you enter into a meditative state faster. For example, don't eat for an hour before you meditate. If you can't avoid eating, take a light meal.

129. The best breathing technique.

The best breathing technique to use while practice mindfulness meditation is deep and slow breaths; breathe in through your nose and out through your mouth.

You can make the shape of an 'O' with your lips in order to exhale; the most important is to part the lips slowly. In this way, your body will begin to relax.

130. Keep your eyes closed.

Of course you don't have to follow this rule, but it can help. In the beginning, your mind could begin trying to fill in the "blank space" with images. This could be a little problem, but do not worry. There is a simple solution – focus on something (e.g. a dot on the wall). Once you begin focusing your attention, your mind will wander from time to time. Gently bring your attention back to the dot as the object of your meditation.

131. How long should you meditate to get results?

There is no rigid rule, but there is a general answer – you should meditate as long as you are comfortable doing so. For beginners, it is recommended to meditate between 3 to 5 minutes. It may seem like a short amount of time, but even 5 minutes of good meditation can give you amazing benefits. As time goes by, you will increase your level, and you can meditate for longer periods.

132. Support is very important.

Let your household members and friends know about your intentions to practice mindfulness and meditation. Your family, especially your spouse and parents, can be vital sources of support. You can ask them to join you.

If they won't join you, explain them that you don't want to be disturbed during your practice. It's the least they can do.

133. If you need additional support.

You can write a blog about your journey and share your experiences with like-minded people. You can also share your experience through social media.

In this way, you'll be able to prepare yourself to stick to your meditation practice long enough to see the positive outcome.

134. Observe your thoughts to go beyond them.

Here are a few steps to study your thoughts.

Step 1: Sit quietly; try to follow your thoughts as they come to your mind.

Step 2: Watch how your thinking gets activated only when you take an interest in some thoughts.

Step 3: Remember that you have a free choice not to get attached to your thoughts. As a matter of fact, you have no reason to be afraid of your thoughts.

135. Nothing will change until you do.

"You cannot travel on the path until you become the path itself." – Buddha

A few times a day, remind yourself – Nothing will change until you do. Meditation is designed for everyone, so you have to be persistent and to believe. Meditation works for everyone. You just have to find the right one.

136. Mindfulness meditation reduces stress, anxiety, and depression.

If you cope with stress or suffer from depression, give mindful meditation a chance. Mindfulness keeps your mind sane and protects your brain. If you meditate consistently, you will receive amazing benefits. Doing this daily, you gain skills to manage your stress, anxiety, and depression. This meditation is based on acceptance of living in the present moment. There are no worries in the present moment.

137. Is mindfulness mediation right for you?

When it comes to meditation, it is really important to choose the one that resonates the most with you. How do you know which to choose? There are many types of meditation: Zen meditation, Vipassana meditation, Loving kindness meditation, Mantra (OM) meditation, etc. Of course, the best meditation is the one that works for you.

In terms of mindfulness meditation, it is an adaptation of traditional Buddhist meditation practices such as Vipassana. Actually, the term "Mindfulness" is the western translation for the Buddhist term "Anapanasati", – mindfulness of breathing.

Mindfulness meditation is a great way to get started with meditation and something that most people would be familiar with. If you are looking for a deeper spiritual development, mindfulness meditation may be your first and most important step.

138. You will have the ability to concentrate better.

Once you begin meditating consistently, your thoughts will take it easy and you won't feel like they're running at full speed constantly. You will be able to focus better and solve ongoing problems better.

139. You'll become more positive.

One of the greatest benefits of mindfulness meditation is that you become more positive over time. If you are worried, mindful meditation gives you the opportunity to slow down and observe your negative discouraging thoughts. You can see them from a distance and you may understand their origin and their mechanism of action.

During the day, negative thoughts just happen and you often do not even notice them. While you meditate, you are fully aware of them, you face them, and you understand their function. In this way, you can transform your negative thoughts into positive experiences.

140. An exercise to slow down your thoughts.

This exercise is very simple – Just stop thinking in words and start thinking in pictures. Try to visualize your thoughts instead of verbalizing them and you will considerably slow down them. In this way, you use the brain's right hemisphere and give the brain's left hemisphere a break. The point of meditation is to balance the use of both hemispheres in order to live life to the fullest.

141. Your goal is to reach the state of thoughtless awareness.

Once you reached short moments of complete silence in your mind, just be in that state. As long as you can.

The moment you realize that you are in a state of thoughtless awareness, the silence will break due the thought about being silent. It is a paradox, isn't it?

Over time, you will start to increase these short silent moments. Well done!

142. Your mind is like a movie theatre.

How to achieve detachment? Imagine your mind as a movie theatre. You are a spectator; you don't have any need to control the direction in which the movie goes.

143. Don't try to rush it.

In order to gain benefits from mindful meditation, you should detach yourself from your emotions as well. Here is a simple exercise for you.

Do not suppress your emotions. Let them arise naturally and observe them; at the same time, try to stay detached. This is not easy, but consistent practice will give you results.

144. Mindfulness meditation is a lifestyle choice.

Actually, meditation is our natural state of being. However, this is easier said than done. In practice, it will take years to achieve the next level.

It takes years for Buddhist monks to achieve the state of thoughtless awareness. For us it might be difficult, but it can be achieved for sure.

145. Visualize your success.

Imagine having the power to experience thoughtless awareness; feel it with all your senses. Visualize every day until you experience improvement. Then, focus on your daily routine, develop your mediation skills every day, and don't give up. And then, start all over again; visualize that you are a good meditator and practice meditation again.

"Success is walking from failure to failure with no loss of enthusiasm." – Winston Churchill.

146. Mindfulness goes with a healthy lifestyle.

Here's a practical tip that will help you in making the most of your daily meditation practice. Meditation will improve all areas of your life. When you meditate every day, your lifestyle will become healthier. You should start exercising and eating healthy.

147. Use aroma therapy during meditation.

Mindfulness meditation is not an easy skill to master. Help yourself using this practical advice. Try to light a scented candle. Some little things make a big difference, believe it or not. Give it a try and you'll experience the benefits firsthand.

148. Practice meditation during sunrise.

Try to meditate early in the morning if possible. The best part of the day is during sunrise because it has a lot of positive energy. This is a great preparation for the rest of the day. It makes it easier to apply mindfulness throughout the day.

149. A great way to increase your focus.

Learn to play a musical instrument. It is a great way to increase your focus, which is the key to successful meditation. In this way, you will learn to take care of the things that are important.

150. Avoid common pitfalls.

As we said before, being mindful of your present state of consciousness is very important in order to find peace within yourself. One of the most powerful tools to get to that state of consciousness is mindfulness meditation. However, people often think that meditation requires a long time to do. It is a common mistake. It takes only fifteen minutes per day and you can get incredible benefits. On the other hand, when you are more skilled, you are able to get to that relaxed state for a short period of time. Win-win!

151. Sleep properly to meditate better.

During deep sleep our brain gets its real rest. It is important to provide your body and mind with an optimal balance of sleep and meditation. We should sleep 8 hours daily to have a healthy mind and body. Remember, if you don't sleep enough, you will not be able to meditate.

152. Spiritual growth for a higher consciousness.

In addition to meditation practice, you should study other related ideas such as holy books, prayer, yoga, and so on. By living the spiritual life, it will be easier for you to meditate. In this way, you are constantly growing in your wisdom.

153. The art of self-reflection.

Everyday self-reflection is a great way to monitor your progress in meditation. "Am I a little better than yesterday?" is a good question to ask yourself frequently. Try to learn something new every day and you will experience progress. When you improve your meditation and mindfulness skills, you will be better in self-reflection.

154. Practice non-attachment.

What does it mean to let go? Non-attachment is one of the keys to a happy and healthy life. It will help you develop a spiritual lifestyle that will ensure that you will live your life to the fullest. Mindfulness meditation is a great way to practice non-attachment. Try to meditate on the attachment by itself. Think of all the things you attach yourself to, including the current and former attachments; you can make a list. Then, meditate on each thing from the list.

You will see into the true nature of your attachments; then, you can easily let them go. Afterward, you can see ways in which you can break your attachments.

155. Develop an open mind.

"You have your way. I have my way. As for the right way, the correct way, and the only way, it does not exist." – Friedrich Nietzsche.

If you are eager to improve your daily meditation, you should develop an open mind. Here are a few tips to learn about perspectives that are different from your own.

a. Explore other belief systems.

b. Read a lot. People who read a lot are more likely to be open-minded.

c. Learning to trust yourself.

d. Learn to embrace changes and new ideas.

Remember – open mind is a focus mind. Therefore, there are good reasons to embrace the power of mindfulness meditation.

156. Meditation is not a religion.

Whether you are spiritual, religious, agnostic, or atheist, meditation is for everyone. You don't need to be a hippie or to live in the mountains. You don't have to be even a spiritualist to reap obvious benefits of mindfulness meditation.

If you are looking for a method of awakening your spirit to live a happier life, mindfulness meditation can help you. Then, if you just need some relax and stress relief, practice mindfulness meditation. Think like this – mindfulness meditation is a life changing skill.

157. Mindfulness meditation on your personal development journey.

Mindfulness meditation is a useful and reliable tool on your personal development journey. In fact, it is hard to imagine personal development without self-analysis, introspection, mindfulness, and meditation.

158. Follow your passion.

"I would rather die of passion than of boredom." —Vincent van Gogh

It is important to do what you enjoy the most. Follow your hobbies and try to enjoy every moment of your life.

Mindfulness and meditation require the mind of the moment. Enjoy it!

159. Learning to trust yourself.

When we are "in the present moment", we're focusing on what's happening in our life right now and here. We're not worried about what did happen especially about what might happen. And we learn to trust yourself and our inner wisdom. When you know yourself, you can trust yourself. In order to truly know yourself, you should meditate. Easy as A-B-C!

160. Keep your priorities clear.

"It's not enough to be busy; so are the ants. The question is: what are we busy about?" – Henry David Thoreau

In order to live the life you love, you should set your priorities. This is what mindfulness is about. Here are a few tips.

    a.   Ask yourself: Am I devoted to my life right now?

    b.   Make sure to "scrape away" all of the distractions that separate you from your passion.

    c.   Take a break and think of what is really important to you.

    d.   What is it that I want? Write it down.

161. Make healthier choices.

Mindfulness and meditations bring wonderful things into your life. Thanks to your practice, you become aware of your everyday choices. You start exercising and eating healthier. Over time, your unhealthy habits such as drinking alcohol or smoking disappear. In fact, you will live in the moment. Happiness indeed.

162. How easy is it to be mindful?

Mindful meditation, at its core, is easy. However, it's easier said than done; it takes time and patience. It also requires us to move through the pain in our lives. Believe it or not, unless you're living in the present moment, you are suffering. Thus, mindfulness meditation is really worth the time and effort. It is much better than being unhappy and miserable.

163. How to find your inner peace?

"He who lives in harmony with himself lives in harmony with the world." – Marcus Aurelius.

There are plenty of things around us that separate us from our inner peace, and distract us from the now. When you truly think about it, you might realize that you live in a pain. Because of that, you should find your inner peace. Here're a few tips and tricks to do that properly.

a. You should practice patience. And you should believe in process. "I believe in the process. I believe in four seasons. I believe that winter's tough, but spring's coming. I believe that there's a growing season. And I think that you realize that in life, you grow. You get better." – Steve Southerland

b. Think long-term and try to see the bigger picture. Do not be distracted by detail and avoid perfectionism.

c. Try to understand rather than judging everything and everyone.

164. You should know what you want.

Mindfulness meditation will help you to discover your true aspirations and dreams. It will help you to understand yourself better. When you know yourself, you will know what makes you happy. In addition to meditation, you can make a list of your passions. Your mind will become more at ease and rest, so that you can perceive your "real self".

165. There are various approaches to mindfulness meditation.

People have different ideas regarding mindfulness meditation. Some people might believe that meditation is a part of a new age philosophy. Other people connect mindfulness meditation with religions such as Buddhism. Thus, there are different beliefs.

Basically, meditation will bring the mind to a certain state of peace. Counselors, psychologists, spiritual leaders, and more, use mindfulness meditation in their practice. It means that mindfulness meditation is a complex mental process and you can't describe it in a few words.

166. Mistakes are lessons.

Our mistakes can help us to make better choices in the future. It may sound a bit odd, but once you experience the benefits of mindfulness, you will be able to understand what this refers to. This is because meditation move us to mindfulness. Our mind becomes more focused on the present moment and we stop spending time trying to determine what we did wrong in the past.

167. Accept your past.

It happened. There's nothing that you can do regarding this except to live with it. If you continue to live in that past, it won't get you anywhere.

With the help of mindfulness meditation, you become stress free and you have peace with yourself. It helps you to accept your pain, not to fight them, but also put it where it needs to be, which is in your past.

168. There's so much to enjoy.

Basically, having peace with yourself allows you to concentrate on what's around you at the present moment. And it's a wonderful experience. There are so many great things to enjoy! You have a family and friends, you are healthy, you can read this book, etc. Afterward, you are alive. Isn't that wonderful?

169. Everyone has their own experiences.

"You never really know a man until you understand things from his point of view, until you climb into his skin and walk around in it." – Nelle Harper Lee. (To Kill a Mockingbird).

Actually, everyone has a much different perspective on some experiences than other people. Remember – just be yourself, everyone has their own perspective on mindfulness. Move forward and get into the present moment to get the most out of your life.

170. How to develop and increase empathy?

To accept different opinions and lifestyle, and understand someone's choices and desires, you should "Walk a mile in someone's shoes". Mindfulness meditation is known for its great effects on our brains. It is also well known that this practice may encourage empathy.

It's been scientifically proven that a meditation program called "Cognitively-Based Compassion Training", based on ancient Buddhist practices, can improve our relationships and compassion towards other people. The same goes for mindfulness meditation. With the help of mindfulness meditation, you can cultivate kindness toward yourself and other people as well.

171. How to become more self-aware?

"Self-observation is the first step of inner unfolding." – Amit Ray.

After regular practice of mindfulness meditation, we start to know ourselves better. A meditator becomes connected with his/her true self. This implies knowing yourself as both a physical and spiritual being, in touch with everything that is and the whole creation. Make sure not to force concentration of mind. Sit comfortable, relax, and breathe. Everything should come to you by itself.

172. Mindfulness meditation will help you solve your problems.

Don't take this the wrong way, but a happy life doesn't mean a complete 'absence' of all troubles. As a matter of fact, we need "problems" in order to expand our level of awareness.

If you observe your problems during meditation, you will realize: a difference is in our attitude and approach towards problems. Actually, challenges do come and go as long as we are alive. By practicing mindfulness meditation, you can suddenly see your problems as challenges and the opportunities to grow and learn.

173. Mindfulness meditation provides a broader outlook.

Meditation is the core of mindfulness. If you want to become more mindful and conscious, you should cultivate non-judgmental attitude and learn to expand your horizons. You can achieve that by practicing meditation every day. Meditation will help you to broaden your outlook by taking control of your life and reframing your perspective. As a matter of fact, our life is never all or nothing.

174. Learn to pay attention.

If you take a moment to breath, focusing on what you're actually experiencing, you will discover the benefits of mindfulness. In this way, you learn to pay attention to your inner voice and trust your intuition. When you meditate, let go of the need to put in so much effort to achieve concentration. Don't use any force to reach higher states of awareness. Just quiet your mind and listen. And remember – be open to the ideas that will come to you.

175. Achieve a realistic self-confidence.

"Meditation is a way for nourishing and blossoming the divine within you." – Amit Ray

Mindfulness meditation can help you create a strong faith in your abilities. The key is to have a patience to wait until the right opportunity comes to us. It is called your realistic self-confidence. Focus on mindful breathing and allow yourself to believe in your abilities. Breathe and just be.

176. The power of mindfulness meditation.

Regardless of whether we practice mindfulness meditation or not, our subconscious mind communicates information to the conscious mind using our intuition. Mindfulness meditation can connect your subconscious and conscious mind.

The key is to pay attention to that process. You can listen to your intuition thought inspiration, unusual ideas, thought flashes, and so on. You have to be a quiet listener. If you can't hear the answers during meditation, just let it go. The voice of intuition occurs when you least expect it.

177. Restlessness is the nature of the human mind.

What is left behind "mind"? Can we separate mind from thoughts? We cannot separate the ocean from its waves. Likewise, we can't free our mind of its thoughts. Therefore, there is no point in spending our time trying to make our mind completely empty. As a matter of fact, we should understand its nature. Mindfulness meditation can help us to discover and take care of the factors that are responsible for our mental agitation.

178. How to come closer to your true self?

If you are eager to determine how your true self looks like, you should try to do something to experience its presence within yourself. You can use a "process of elimination" to find out what your true self is not. You can find it through mindfulness meditation. Actually, we use the process of elimination in our day-to-day life to separate cause from effect. Therefore, mindfulness meditation implies first-hand experience of your real self.

179. How to find a quiet place?

Sometimes, it seems difficult to find a place for meditation practice. Especially if you have children or pets. You can go to the library and isolate yourself.

You can also try to meditate outdoors. You may find that it is a perfect surroundings for you.

180. How to meditate outdoors?

The Buddha sat beneath a Bodhi tree while meditating. In the western world, reaching the state of mindfulness is the challenging. How about trying to meditate in natural surroundings? Our being resonates with the sound of birds and flowing water, as well as feeling of the breeze. If you are a nature lover, you will love this kind of mindfulness meditation. Here are a few rules:

a. You can sit, stand or walk.

b. Close your eyes.

c. You can focus on the sounds in the environment. You can also focus on one particular sound (e.g. bird song).

d. It is important to experience everything with an open awareness.

181. The benefits of meditating outdoors.

Meditating outdoors can offer a lot of benefits. Deep in the woods, you will be able to clear your mind much easier.

There are so many things to focus. You can look at the clouds or the leaves on the tree. For instance, you can count the leaves to stay focused. Try to meditate in a new environment instead of spend time in a quiet room. Just give it a try.

182. Mindfulness meditation is great for your soul.

"Meditation helps you to grow your own intuitive faculty. It becomes very clear what is going to fulfill you, what is going to help you flower." – Osho.

To be aware of your soul, you have to withdraw your attention from the world outside to the inner self. It is a great way to reach soul enlightenment.

183. Try to establish your mantra.

Repeat the word or phrase (mantra) throughout your meditation. It will provide a point of focus. In the beginning, you can repeat: I am breathing in, I am breathing out. Of course, keep in mind that what works for someone may not work for you. We approach things differently. You should find your way.

184. Exhale stress, inhale peace.

Try this powerful exercise and experience great advantages of mindfulness meditation.

Step 1: Sit comfortably and exclude all distractions. Try your best to calm the mind; do not think about anything else except that moment.

Step 2: Begin breathing. It's supposed to be natural. Slowly and gently, exhale your negativity. Then, slowly and naturally, take a deep breath, inhaling the freshness and peace. Release anything that doesn't serve you; stress, anxiety, worries, tension, etc.

Step 3: Note each breath, without trying to control anything. When you notice mind-wandering, gently (without any judgment) bring your attention back to the breath. Take it easy, this is your own journey, not a competition.

185. Nothing is permanent.

"There is nothing permanent except change." – Heraclitus.

Impermanence is a really big topic. When we are free of the idea of permanence, we can see the beauty of living in the moment. Mindfulness and meditation can help you to accept this concept.

186. Meditation opens your wakeful awareness.

"When meditation is mastered, the mind is unwavering like the flame of a candle in a windless place." – Bhagavad Gita.

Here's a simple exercise you can try right now. Take away your focus from the things that are cluttered in your mind and concentrate on your environment. What do you notice? How do you feel about that?

There is a difference between focused and mindfulness meditation. The first meditation focuses on one thing. Mindfulness meditation is more flexible; your mind can dwell on several things.

187. Decide to stick with it.

To make mindfulness meditation a daily habit, you have to practice. In the beginning, set micro goals; for example, commit to just 3 to 5 minutes a day. Decide to stick with it. Practice it for a month and you'll form your daily meditation habit.

188. One of the goals of mindfulness meditation.

Basically, all types of meditation can help you relax. The mindfulness meditation is a little bit different because you should try to relax while you are totally aware of your surroundings. Have you ever stopped and taken time to observe all the things that you can possibly see? It is so relaxing to be present in the moment. Give it a try!

189. Discover your greatest fulfillment.

One of the greatest things that mindfulness meditation can offer you is that it lets you enjoy a new state of fulfillment. A messy mind doesn't allow you to see your real self and experience fulfillment in your life.

Mindful meditation provides you with numerous states of consciousness. As your fulfillment increases your suffering decreases; your satisfaction with your own life is growing. To practice this state of consciousness, find a comfortable position and think of nothing but your breath. Focus on the way you breathe. Can you feel this expansion of consciousness? Great.

190. Meditations is not a competition.

"Your journey is your journey not a competition." – unknown author. Your job is to find your way, your own and unique path because you are special. You are unique and there is not a person in the whole world who can compare to you. Therefore, you should create your own style and go at your own pace.

191. An exercise to keep you on track.

When you learn to turn your attention inwards, you can enjoy the benefits of mindfulness meditation. Like most good things, it is not easy. It requires practice, but that doesn't mean it's impossible. Quite the contrary, mindfulness meditation is for everyone. Basically, you must be gentle and encouraging to yourself when you are learning to meditate.

Here's a great exercise to keep you on track. Choose a comfortable position. Inhale as much as you can or until your stomach contracts inwards; hold for as long as you can. Focus on breathing in and holding, then, breathing out and holding.

192. An easy 3-minute mindfulness meditation.

This short mindfulness meditation lasts three minutes and you can do this anywhere. Here's how it goes:

Step 1: Sit on a chair in a comfortable upright balanced position. Close your eyes.

Step 2: Focus on your breath. Slowly and gently breathe in and breathe out.

Step 3: When you notice your thoughts wandering astray, gently guide your focus back to your breath. When you are ready, slowly open your eyes; you will feel refreshed.

193. An exercise – count up to five.

This exercise will help you stay focused for longer.

Inhale by counting up to 5, or until your stomach contracts inwards; hold, counting up to 5. Focus on breathing in and holding, and, then, breathing out and holding.

194. Everything that has a beginning has an ending.

"Everything that has a beginning has an ending. Make your peace with that and all will be well." – Jack Kornfield, Buddha's Little Instruction Book. With the help of meditation, we become aware of this simple fact.

195. Motivate yourself.

You must be encouraging and gentle to yourself. You should overcome difficulties that keep you from your daily practice. If you have a busy lifestyle, it can be tricky. If you do not have time for meditation, you need meditation. It sounds weird, but it is true. If your thoughts are rushing, don't worry. It happens. Motivate yourself and avoid distractions as much as possible.

When things don't go your way, don't get frustrated. Don't rush it and keep practicing.

196. Try to change position during meditation.

Getting into a routine can be difficult. Do not try to force things to happen, accept the situation with equanimity. Instead, change your posture and choose the one that suits you.

"Don't force things, let life decide what happens. If it's meant to be, then it will be. Just wait and see." – Unknown author.

197. How to exit meditation.

Slowly and gently open your eyes. Don't rush it and take some time to just be there. Allow your thoughts to run free and spend some time to feel gratitude for being alive. Further, you can say "Thank you" or you can say your favorite positive affirmations. In the beginning, try guided meditations and you will learn how to exit meditation properly. Afterward, when you move back into this world, you can feel the benefits of mindfulness meditation in every aspect of your life.

198. Loving-kindness meditation.

To prepare for your meditation, take a few deep breaths. Step 1: As we said before, focus on this cycle of breathing in, holding, breathing out, and holding. As your breathing slows down, you will slow down your mind and control racing thoughts.

Step 2: Bring to your mind your beloved one; notice your feelings for them arise in your whole body.

Step 3: Then, let go of that person and keep in your awareness only the feelings. Bring yourself to mind and ask yourself: "How can I love you even more?

199. How to stick with the habit of meditation I?

If you are serious about your practice, don't miss even a single day. Three days in a row should be your maximum allowance. Take this advice seriously if you tend to turn mindfulness meditation into a habit.

200. How to stick with the habit of meditation II?

If you can't stop mental chatter and you are thinking about giving up, consider this trick. You can observe the thoughts instead of trying to slow them down! Yes, it is hard to tame your monkey mind. Sometimes, it's nearly impossible to enjoy the present moment, as well as mindfulness meditation. Therefore, try to observe each and every thought without judgment and with equanimity. Meditation and mindfulness practice are the most effective ways you can use to tame your monkey mind, but it takes time to realize that you rule your thoughts and not vice-versa.

201. Practice makes better.

If you can't slow down your mind, consider the following method. The universe is infinite and it is expanding. Imagine that you're moving through our galaxy. You are traveling near the planets, meteors and other stars. At the end, you can see a glass wall. Picture the black space, which is an illusion. Every time you have intrusive thoughts, go right back to that imaginary black space and the glass wall. Look back at the stars and then turn to face the black space. Remember – practice makes better.

202. Mindfulness on sitting in the garden.

As we said before, you can practice mindfulness while doing any task. Here's a great exercise to keep in track of your practice.

Step 1: Start by sitting in a spot in a quiet garden. Then, take a deep breath in, and exhale. Repeat this three times.

Step 2: Try to be fully aware of your surroundings. What sounds do you hear? Are there insects around? Look at the Sun, plants, sky, and clouds. Observe them like a child, without labeling.

Step 3: When you notice your mind wandering, gently, with a lot of love for yourself, bring it back to the task.

Step 4: Thank all these elements for supporting your life: The Sun, air, water, plants, and so on.

203. You deserve good things.

Many people don't live their lives to the fullest because they think that they don't deserve good things. Mindfulness meditation will help you to raise the awareness of your true worth. Once you realize that, you will have less self-sabotage in your life.

"You yourself, as much as anybody in the entire universe, deserve your love and affection."

– Buddha

204. Do you know how to love yourself?

It all begins with you. When you start meditating, you start to understand yourself much better. Mindfulness meditation will help you to accept and embrace your experiences, both good and bad. And learn to live with them. That's you. That' your life and you have nothing to be ashamed of. Likewise, you do not have any reason to blame yourself and do not love yourself. In this way, you start to love yourself unconditionally.

205. Learn to love yourself.

Mindfulness meditation will help you to understand self-love, including self-acceptance, self-awareness, and respect for yourself. You should overcome negative beliefs about yourself. Nothing is more important than loving yourself.

"You're always with yourself, so you might as well enjoy the company." – Diane Von Furstenberg.

206. The mindfulness guide for the super busy.

When it comes to mindfulness, what does it mean when talking about "pain"?

"Pain" doesn't have to be physical or emotional. It could be anxiety and self-sabotage in your day-to-day life. If you are busy, you are constantly under the stress, although it doesn't seem like it. Just because you don't feel the struggle in a direct emotional way, that doesn't mean it's not exist. Mindfulness meditation will help you to take your power back and live your life to the fullest.

207. Forget on multi-tasking.

How to enjoy your life and strive for your goals at the same time? Is that possible? It may seem contradictory, but by cultivating mindfulness, it can help you fulfill your dreams.

The idea is simple – focusing on one task at a time is much more effective than multi-tasking. Therefore, use mindfulness meditation to focus on one goal at a time.

208. Mindfulness and productivity.

If you focus on what you're doing right now, you will be more productive. When you're mindful, you are more creative and more effective. By relaxing your mind, you can learn to embrace each moment so that you take advantage of each and every situation.

209. What else do you have than the present moment?

What else do you have than the present moment? The past is over; the future doesn't exist. The past and the futures are concepts; we perceive time like this in our dimension. When you meditate, there is no time. There is only pure consciousness, which is eternal.

After all, Henry David Thoreau said, "You must live in the present, launch yourself on every wave, find your eternity in each moment."

210. The awakening of the consciousness.

"I regard consciousness as fundamental. I regard matter as derivative from consciousness. We cannot get behind consciousness. Everything that we talk about, everything that we regard as existing, postulating consciousness." – Max Planck, theoretical physicist.

Many people live in a "deep sleep". They live on autopilot. Mindfulness meditation can help us raise our consciousness. Heightened consciousness, not only brings you self-awareness, but it can have a huge impact on the world around you.

211. Everything is in your mind.

By meditating, you can achieve calmness and serenity, so that you will be able to open yourself to all possibilities. Nothing is really good or bad by itself. Once you understand that, you'll be able to go out and enjoy your life to the fullest. You will be more in tune with everything that can happen.

212. Turn negative experiences into positive life lessons.

Mindfulness will bring enrichment to your life. It doesn't mean that you won't have the painful experiences. In fact, pain and struggle can remind us to enjoy life even more.

We experience ups and downs constantly; by practicing mindfulness, we learn to turn our negative experiences into the positive life lessons.

213. Go beyond traditional thought.

When you get into mindfulness meditation, you can view things much differently than the majority of people. You go beyond traditional thought and expand your perspective. This is one of the greatest benefits of mindfulness meditation.

214. Widen your horizons.

When you have more peace in yourself, your viewpoint is going to change. It can be challenging for you. You should find your own perspective. After all, it is the only thing you have access to. Living in the present moment will make it easier for you to widen your horizons.

215. Embrace other points of view.

This is considered one of the hardest things that people face when they try to improve their relationships. If you can listen and consider other points of view, you are blessed. That's amazing characteristics that everyone does not have. Cultivate that quality by practicing mindfulness meditation.

At the same time, you learn to cultivate empathy and lasting emotional control. Win-win!

216. Accept full responsibility for yourself and your life.

Accepting personal responsibility may seem scary at first glance. I am responsible for everything! What do you really mean by that? What does it mean to be responsible? It means that you accept that you are the absolute creator of your life.

When you get into mindfulness meditation, you realize that simple truth. Without practicing mindfulness, it can be tough to accept. The problem isn't that life is unfair, the problem is your perspective of life. The sooner you understand this, the better your life will be.

217. Our reality is a kind of illusion.

According to a theory in quantum physics, your reality is a kind of illusion; it exists only when you are observing it. Yes, it's a blow-minding theory, but it's been scientifically proven. Mindfulness is about perception as well, right?

218. Suffering is completely optional.

Is the glass half empty or half full? It's your choice. How do you see your presence on this planet?

"Pain is inevitable. Suffering is optional. Say you're running and you think, 'Man, this hurts, I can't take it anymore'. The 'hurt' part is an unavoidable reality, but whether or not you can stand anymore is up to the runner himself." – Haruki Murakami.

219. Take a nap a few times a day.

A few times a day, go to a quiet and dark place. Shut the door and lie down. This daily habit will significantly improve your mindfulness practice.

NASA scientists have proven that a 26-minute nap improved pilot performance by 34 percent and alertness by 54 percent.

220. Yoga and mindfulness meditation.

Yoga class is a great way to become more aware of the present moment. Mindful yoga is a great practice of deliberate movement.

As one of the main meditation postures, Savasana can help you to stay on track with your mindfulness meditation practice.

Step 1: Lie on your back with your feet about 18 inches apart; your arms should be at your sides a few inches away from the torso, with the palms up.

Step 2: Open to the breath and its various qualities such as deep or shallow, fast or slow.

Step 3: Then, start to scan your body. When your mind starts wandering, gently bring it back to the breath and the body.

221. Body scan meditation.

Actually, the body scan is a component of mindfulness meditation. Just focus your attention around the body, by observing any sensations that you become aware of. You can use your favorite meditation posture, but it is recommended to lie down on a mat or your bed, and do nothing. Great! You should do this exercise step by step, while becoming aware of all sensations in your body, with mindful attitudes.

You can start from your head; then, move down the body. This practice trains your mind to move from a wide to narrow focus of attention. Try to start with a guided meditation to gain insights into the practice. Good luck!

222. Movement meditation.

This is the type of mindfulness meditation, known as physical mind-body exercise. It includes practices such as T'ai chi, Qigong, Yoga, etc. It involves focusing on your bodily sensations, mindfully watching, and breathing. It also includes letting go of thoughts and emotions that arise as you practice.

223. Mindfulness walking meditation.

This is the combination of slow walking meditation and a physical mind-body exercise. This kind of meditation is usually done much slower than normal walking; it also includes breathing, as well as specific focusing practice. Unlike a sitting meditation, there is much more interaction with the outside world. It brings well-being benefits. There are several types of walking meditation such as Theravada walking meditation, Zen walking meditation, etc.

When it comes to mindfulness walking meditation, this is an adaptation of Buddhist walking meditation. Your aim is to focus on sensations and perceptions of the present moment. Like it or not, all we have is the present moment.

224. Tips to make mindfulness walking meditation easier.

a. First and foremost, keep your awareness engaged in the experience of walking.

b. It is important to be aware of the location in space. Feel the air temperature and listen to the sounds around you.

c. Focus your attention on the variety of sensations and perceptions of the present moment.

225. Mindfulness walking meditation as a type of open monitoring meditation.

Open monitoring meditation is the process of monitoring of the experiences (internal or external) from moment to moment. Actually, instead of focusing our attention on certain object or breathing, we try to keep it open, monitoring all aspects of our current experience. We observe thoughts and emotions as internal experiences, as well as smell, sounds and objects as external experience. If you are looking for dynamic meditation techniques, give this meditation a try.

226. Mindfulness walking meditation and body scan.

Feel the movement of your muscles and your feet touching the ground. Gradually pay attention to every part of your body. Then, gradually and slowly, scan every part of your body. Observe the sensations as you walk. For some people, it is easier to practice walking meditation, especially if you're inexperienced.

227. Breathing space meditation.

This meditation is great when you experience stressful and difficult situations. You can practice this meditation a few times a day. The key to successful mindfulness meditation is to create a full awareness of your current experience instead of avoiding it. This three-minute meditation is a brief practice and it can be used when we want to come into the present moment quickly.

Step 1: Close your eyes. Then, ask yourself: What thoughts are around?

Step 2: Instead of trying to push your emotions and thoughts away, you should notice and observe them. In this way, you become aware of your experiences.

Step 3: Then, try not to think about anything at all, for 15 seconds.

Step 4: Focus on your breathing; notice when the breath is moving in, and when the breath is moving out.

Step 5: Then, try not to think about anything at all, for 15 seconds.

Step 6: Allow your awareness to expand to the entire body; bring your full attention to the entire body. When you are ready, open your eyes.

228. Mindfulness mountain meditation.

This is a great meditation to cultivate stability, as well as feel more centered. It is recommended to do this practice in a sitting position.

Step 1: Once you find a position of stability, close your eyes, bringing awareness to your breath.

Step 2: Then, allow an image to form in your mind; the image of the most beautiful mountain you have ever imagined or seen. Notice its magnificent, its beauty, and sturdiness.

Step 3: Now bring the mountain into your own body. In other words, your body becomes one with the mountain; you become the mountain with its stillness and the massiveness. The lofty peak is your head. Your shoulders become the sides of the mountain. Your legs are rooted to the ground.

Step 4: This mountain (you) just sits, experiencing each moment. As you sit, you are seeing how night follows day and vice versa. You can feel the Sun and its warm, you can feel the rain on your skin, as well as a mountain breeze and wind. Magnificent!

In your life, you experience changes constantly; you have your own periods of day and night, i.e. the light and darkness. By becoming the mountain, you can use its energy to fill each and every moment with strength, stability, and mindfulness.

229. Lake mindfulness meditation.

This meditation is similar to previous. Breathe as the lake and feel as the lake, allowing your mind to be receptive for the experiences of the present moment. This mindful meditation can help you to allow the experiences to be just as they are.

230. Expanding awareness meditation.

This mindfulness meditation technique allows us to be in touch with where we are here and right now.

Although you can practice it in your favorite position, it is sitting meditation in general. This technique involves focusing on your breath, sounds, thoughts, and feelings; you become aware of whatever is most predominant in your conscious and subconscious mind. There are a few types of expanding awareness meditation:

- Mindfulness of breath meditation,
- Mindfulness of thoughts meditation,
- Mindfulness of feelings meditation,
- Mindfulness of body meditation,
- Mindfulness of sounds meditation.

231. Mindfulness of breath meditation.

Mindfulness meditation itself is a mirror of your personal development. It is about waking up from your longtime dream, perhaps a nightmare. How does it work? Focus your attention on your breathing, in and out. And do not forget, each time the mind starts wandering, gently, with a lot of love for yourself, bring it back.

232. Mindfulness of thoughts meditation.

Not knowing that you are on autopilot is what the Buddhists call "ignorance". Once you realize that you think and act on autopilot, you become mindfully aware.

Being aware of the constant chatter of the mind is the first step to "enlightenment". Then, you can create a distance between yourself and your thoughts. Great! Yes, it is easy to suggest, but hard to do. No worries, just allow each and every thought to come and go, at their own pace, without attaching to them. That's it!

233. Mindfulness of feelings meditation.

"The best and most beautiful things in the world cannot be seen or even touched. They must be felt with the heart." – Helen Keller

A cultivation of wakefulness is a long-term process, but it is not impossible. This waking up goes hand in hand with wisdom. Mindfulness of feelings meditation is about watching our feelings as an indifferent spectator; you stop constantly judging them and that's it. Our feelings arise and fall constantly. And pretty soon, they will be replaced by another feeling, and so on. Therefore, there is no reason to label them, still less to attach to them.

234. Mindfulness of body meditation.

This meditation technique involves the physical sensation in our body from moment to moment or at the present moment. To practice this technique, you should imagine every part of your body as a separate component. Spend some time being aware of each part of your body. Then, relax any part until you become totally relaxed in the present moment. If you are inexperienced in meditation, try a guided meditation.

235. Mindfulness of sounds meditation.

This type of mindfulness meditation means paying attention to sounds, in a particular way, nonjudgmentally.

How about background sounds such as traffic noise, murmuring voices, bird songs, and so on. You should observe these emotions without attachment and judgment, but with great awareness. In addition to the background sounds, you can listen to melodic sounds, excluding any emotional response. It can be tricky, but practice makes you better.

236. Mindfulness meditation and sudden sounds.

Sudden sounds can interrupt you and your state of deep relaxation. For instance, you can hear dogs barking. This is completely normal: the noise is a part of every meditation practice. Don't get frustrated, the barking is not going to go away because you fight them in your head. When you commit yourself to paying attention to certain sounds, new possibilities open up!

237. Listen to the silence.

"You need to train yourself to be comfortable with silence, particularly when dealing with cultures that respect silence more than we do in the West." – Tony Buon, The Leadership Coach

Dealing with a noise can be challenging. However, if you learn to listen to silence, you will be able to hear that stillness actually speaks. For instance, you just have to capture the moments between words and musical tones. A melody consists of different tones, as well as short periods of silence.

238. Encounter each moment with clarity.

By practicing mindfulness, you may understand that our emotional storms, feelings, and crisis are subject to change. We tend to take it all personally, and that's our mistake. Mindfulness meditation can teach you this truth, and much more if you can let it in.

239. Record your past experiences of mindfulness meditation.

To stay on track, you can record your improvement and overall experience. Mindfulness is the art of conscious living, but it requires discipline. However, it becomes better by practicing mindfulness meditation on a daily basis. If you record your experience, you will easily motivate and empower yourself.

240. Capturing your moments.

If we live in an automatic mode of unawareness, it's hard to notice the experiences in the present moment. The mind easily escapes from the present moment, so that we need to keep our attention focused. By practicing mindfulness meditation and paying attention, we can capture moments. In this way, we cultivate mindfulness day by day.

241. Are you ready for mindfulness meditation?

There is a proverb, "When the student is ready the teacher will appear."

Many people are not ready to go on a spiritual journey. Actually, there is a time for everything; we have to come to it at the right time in the life. You should be ready to listen to your inner wisdom and intuition, without having the need to go anywhere. This is not an easy job. Regardless of whether you are a very beginner or you have been practicing meditation for years, you should be ready for the spirit of mindfulness.

242. Remember who you are.

If you can awaken consciousness right here and right now, little by little, you will open your heart in all parts. This applies both to our physical world and all Higher Worlds. First, and foremost, you should understand that you are asleep; it is very difficult to remember who you really are. This is the key to spiritual happiness, so that any kind of mindfulness meditation can be helpful here.

243. Your deepest soul essence.

Who you are? In this present moment? If you are not sure, but you are struggling in your everyday life, it's time to reveal your true self. Mindfulness meditation can help you to engage in meditation practice and discover the bloom of the present moment.

Where are you going? What is your deepest soul essence?

"It takes courage to grow up and become who you really are." – E.E. Cummings.

244. Express your uniqueness.

Mindfulness meditation will help us to discover our true values and aspirations. You start enjoying each and every moment you spend with yourself. You begin to feel a deep respect for your uniqueness. Once you express your uniqueness, great things are going to happen.

"You are the only you God made... God made you and broke the mold." – Max Lucado.

245. Mindfulness meditation is liberating work.

When you are practicing mindfulness meditation, you stop dwelling on the past and concerning about the future. Mindfulness meditation is a way to take charge of the quality of your own experiences, including every aspect of your life. It liberates you from the stress and anxiety, as well as the thoughts that do not serve you. Take a short walk, and breathe; it will help you get centered.

246. Shift into the "being mode".

When you start practicing mindfulness meditation, you notice that things get simpler. You are able to watch the situation in this moment, without trying to fight or change it at all. Just breathe and let be. Things will sort themselves out all right. Give it a try.

247. The truth liberates.

Mindfulness is not just a way to a happier life, it is also a way to find out the truth about yourself! The truth, whatever it is, can liberate us. Mindfulness meditation can help you to discover self-knowledge, self-acceptance and self-love.

248. Mindfulness meditation is enlightening work.

Mindfulness meditation allows us to see more clearly; we start to understand more deeply ourselves and our environment. This practice may include deep emotions, such as fear, wounded-ness, sadness, and anger; however, it is empowering, mindfulness will help us to cope with these emotions. On the other hand, it helps us to appreciate feelings such as happiness, serenity, cheerfulness that often go unacknowledged. Here's a tip for you: rest in silence in order to reconnect with your higher-self.

249. Taking things for granted.

"It's not a bad idea to occasionally spend a little time thinking about things you take for granted. Plain everyday things." – Evan Davis

There are too many amazing things we take for granted on a daily basis. Our freedom, a bed to sleep in, a roof over our heads, the Sun as a source of life, your workspace, someone who loves you, and so on. Remind yourself of these "common" things every morning when you wake up. Arguably, paying attention in this way, open up new horizons for clarity, determination, creativity, better choices, and wisdom. This is the power of mindfulness living!

250. Morning mindfulness meditation.

In the morning, don't hone in on your to-do list first. After freshening up in the bathroom, consider meditating for 15 to 20 minutes. Try to stick to the morning meditation routine and you will see awesome benefits. You can simply go back to your bed, close your eyes and breathe. People who stick to this routine claim that it has a huge positive impact on all areas of their day. Happiness indeed!

251. Mindfulness is more complex than being awake.

We live in the modern world and our mind acts like a wild monkey, jumping from one thought to another. By starting mindful meditation practice, you become more aware of your thoughts and you have a thirst for knowledge. Because of that, you start developing an interest in holy books and other spiritual books, as well as philosophy. Mindfulness meditation go hand in hand with prayer as well. Arguably, mindfulness meditation may have an effect on our psychological health. Therefore, learning mindfulness is a complex task, it is an integrative, mind-body based approach.

252. Remember that mindfulness meditation is a practice.

It will be hard moments, but they are part of the life, too. Mindfulness meditation is practice, but it means that you don't have to force yourself to be relaxed or non-judgmental. You don't have to improve anything, including yourself. Remember, we are not trying to get anywhere else. In this way, life becomes your meditation teacher. Try to get some emotional distance. After and before meditation, rest in silence in order to reconnect with your higher-self.

253. Mindfulness and compassion.

"The purpose of human life is to serve, and to show compassion and the will to help others." – Albert Schweitzer.

When you cultivate a non-judgmental awareness, you cultivate compassion as well. Compassion brings happiness to our lives. You can practice to stop for a while and try to listen and understand others. Like any other good thing, you should make it a daily practice.

Here is a practical exercise. Take a walk and just breathe, gently and deeply; bring to mind a difficult person or the person with whom you are in conflict. Try to understand their behavior rather than criticize. Try to empathize and see the person from another point of view. "You never really know a man until you understand things from his point of view, until you climb into his skin and walk around in it." – Lee, Harpe, To Kill a Mockingbird,

254. Listen to other people.

Here's a simple exercise to practice compassion towards other people, as a key component of mindfulness. Forget complicated philosophy and think about compassion every time when you interact with other people. Try to understand their needs by listening them very carefully.

"If you want others to be happy, practice compassion. If you want to be happy, practice compassion." – Dalai Lama

255. How to deepen your compassion.

Sometimes, we have a distorted view of the world around us. Consequently, we often cannot see people as they really are. Here's a great exercise to deepen your compassion toward yourself and others. Look at other people carefully; ask yourself: "Am I really seeing them or I just have thoughts about them."

256. How to shift our mind toward compassion?

Suffering is an inevitable part of life. Every person suffers, more or less. There are many things over which we have no control. Suffering is a part of being human and it is completely normal. Mindfulness meditation can learn us to embrace negative emotions and turn them into life lessons.

However, we can create a kinder world. We can understand other people and shift our mind toward compassion. It is the core of mindfulness meditation practice.

257. Mindfulness and curiosity.

If you are eager for new opportunities, you must be curious. If you want to gain some new knowledge, curiosity is a precondition. How can you improve curiosity with mindfulness meditation? In order to succeed, you should feed your curiosity every day.

Keep asking yourself questions such as: "What am I noticing now?"; "Where do I feel positive emotions in my body?"; "Where do I feel negative ones?". During meditation practice, you can step back and observe what is happening at the present moment. You should be interested in whatever is showing up, both positive and negative.

258. How to develop curiosity?

Throughout the day, stop, take a deep breath and ask yourself: "What am I noticing in my thoughts right now?"

Of course, by practicing mindfulness and meditation, we gain more flexible attitudes in our life and we understand that we have a lot of choices.

259. Mindfulness and acceptance.

Actually, acceptance is a synonym for mindfulness. When you are mindful and you are aware of the present moment, you are here, in acceptance. Keep in mind that acceptance isn't acquiescence. Do not confuse these terms. Acquiescence gives you a sense of helplessness. Acceptance is your personal choice. Life is not perfect, there are many situations that you were not planning. Bad things happen and that's it. However, acceptance is better than resistance. Mindfulness meditation is one of the best practices to learn acceptance and be happier with your choices.

36 THINGS MINDFUL PEOPLE DO DIFFERENTLY EVERY DAY

Happy people shine like diamonds.

Many studies have shown that practicing mindfulness regularly allows you to see the best perspective on life. Mindful people make the best of everything. And they feel great because of that. Mindful people are happy people, and happy people shine like diamonds. If you are kind to someone else, that person is likely to feel good as well. In this way, you spread happiness to those around you. Happiness indeed!

260. Get dressed mindfully.

Getting dressed in the morning is a great opportunity to practice mindfulness. Mindful people are aware of this.

Step 1: Stop for a moment and take a deep breath. Then, take a few mindful breaths.

Step 2: Now, proceed with your activity as if it is the only important thing. What does it feel like? Sound like? Smell it feel any confusion, any stress, and anxiety. Keep your attention on what you are doing, breathing mindfully.

Step 3: Your mind will probably start to wander at some point. Gently return it to the present moment. Remember, mindfulness is a wonderful journey, not a destination.

261. Mindful people take walks.

You should know that simply going for a walk can be perfect way to slow down your racing mind and gain new perspective.

You can practice slow walking meditation, which is also a great physical exercise. This kind of meditation is usually done much slower than normal walking; it also includes breathing.

262. They like to draw and paint.

It is well known that the art is therapy. Art brings you into the present moment. You are working quietly dwelling in the present moment. You don't have to hurry on to the next thing.

Let painting or drawing be your time for letting go of all doing. You can listen to some soft music; pay attention to your current project and just let it flow. You should create a space without expectations and without judgments.

263. They boost their self-confidence.

Nobody is perfect. The sooner you accept that, your life will be better. Perfectionism drains your energy and hope, by killing your self-esteem. Someone can have all the knowledge in the world, but it means nothing without the confidence. Mindful people take actions every day to build their self-esteem.

And remember – whatever you do, trust yourself!

"As soon as you trust yourself, you will know how to live." – Johann Wolfgang von Goethe.

264. Mindful people forgive themselves all the time.

"Be gentle first with yourself if you wish to be gentle with others." – Lama Yeshe.

Sometimes, it is quite normal, somebody is going to get hurt through our actions. Mindful people are aware of that, so they learn to forgive themselves. How to forgive yourself? Here are a few tips to follow:

a. Remember that you are a good person and accept yourself.

b. You should talk to someone. Professional help is a good choice.

c. You are your own best friend. You can imagine that your child, parent or best friend had done what you did. What would you tell them? The same advice goes for you.

265. Childlike curiosity may inspire you.

"All children are artists. The problem is how to remain an artist once he grows up." – Pablo Picasso

Everyone can develop the state of being more present in their lives. Mindful people are aware of that. Curiosity helps us to get back in touch with the wonders of life. Children are endlessly curious, so try to increase childlike behavior by using mindfulness meditation. Children live in the present, they have no concerns about being cool, they lose themselves in play, etc. Smile and be like them!

266. They see the wonders of life.

As Plato noticed, "Beauty lies in the eyes of the beholder", we all have different perspectives. Believe it or not, mindful people are convinced that life is beautiful. They see the wonders of life. They also claim that we have everything we need to succeed. And the universe has big plans for us. Happiness indeed!

267. Every new sunrise is a chance to learn more about themselves.

Mindful people are convinced that every new day is new opportunity to grow and learn. Many studies have shown that practicing mindfulness regularly allows you to see the best perspective on life.

And remember – you are good enough. You always do the best you can. Period.

268. Mindful people choose happiness.

"I think, the very motion of our life is towards happiness." – Dalai Lama, The Art of Happiness.

Happiness is a choice not a destination. Mindful people welcome joy, courage and optimism into their life. Happiness must become very reasonable goal for you. Your goal is to find fulfillment in your life. Mindfulness practice allows you to train your mind to be happier.

269. Mindful people choose activities wisely.

Mindful people are constantly discovering new ideas about more meaningful life. Ask yourself the following question, as often as you can: What sorts of activities make me feel better? In this way, you start choosing your activities wisely and carefully. It's not just about one thing, it's about a range of different activities that together lead to your overall well-being. All these activities should work together for you.

270. Mindful people hold their emotions lightly.

Mindful people learn to let go of things and emotions that don't really matter. They know that life consists of both positive and negative emotions. Therefore, they don't take themselves too seriously and they have a greater emotional awareness. This is not namby-pamby nonsense. This is a scientifically proven fact.

271. A good and supportive friend.

They are always ready to help others who need it. Mindfulness people practice compassion and empathy. On the other hand, they like spending time with friends and having fun as well. According to research in positive psychology, mindfulness can help us to cultivate trust, and learn to be generous and grateful. If you fancy being like that, you will be able to achieve it by being thankful for your friendships.

272. Mindful people embrace vulnerability.

Since they started practicing mindfulness, they see things in a different way. Yes, it takes courage to be open and vulnerable. In this way, they develop courage and trust. People usually avoid being vulnerable. You should know that being vulnerable is not a weakness. A great idea is to practice mindfulness and meditation in order to embrace vulnerability. Afterward, you begin to trust yourself and other people.

273. They are constantly growing wiser.

Mindful people try identifying their true values and moving towards them. It causes them to feel more satisfied with their lives and grow each and every they. Not knowing our true value is like not knowing the direction of the trip. Through a mindfulness practice you can train your mind to think wiser and make wiser decisions. Mindful people have a better understanding of the meaning of life, they place an emphasis on personal growth rather than on superficial things.

274. Learn to grow from a crisis.

They are strong because they take care of themselves. Here's a great exercise for you.

Step 1: Stop what you're doing; try to re-focus. Do not forget mindful breathing. This will provide oxygen to your body and help you to relax.

Step 2: Pay attention to your current experience. How are you feeling? Write it down.

Step 3: Count up to 10. Thus, you walk away from the situation and allow yourself to consider the options.

275. Mindful people listen to other people.

Good listening skill has been found to be one of the key factors in great relationships. Here're practical tips to help you become a better listener.

a. Look at the speaker and keep the eye-contact.

b. Avoid multitasking and distractions. Keep your phone away, and turn off the TV.

c. Don't interrupt other people.

"I like to listen. I have learned a great deal from listening carefully. Most people never listen." – Ernest Hemingway.

276. Mindful people listen to their inner voice.

"The more you trust your intuition, the more empowered you become, the stronger you become, and the happier you become." – Gisele Bundchen.

It's easy to listen to your intuition when you live in the present moment. By practicing mindfulness, you learn to hear your inner voice better and become aware of your intuitive powers.

277. The power of positive emotions.

Positive emotions can boost your long-term well-being. Feelings such as love, hope, gratitude, serenity, and inspiration fall into this category. If you can enjoy the present moment, you will be able to enjoy these emotions to the fullest. Actually, the present moment is an essential element of wellbeing. By practicing mindfulness, you become aware of positive emotions, without getting attached to them.

278. They are fully engaged in an activity.

They do one thing at a time. When they are walking, they walk. When they are working, they work. They do each and every task, regardless of whether it is small or big, with all of their attention. This is the key to mindfulness and happier life. In this way, you will be able to develop the skills of concentration and attention. You will be able to focus on your task and get everything done. Happiness indeed!

279. Mindful people daydream.

Mindful people love daydreaming, but they don't waste time thinking about a future that nobody cannot predict. Awareness of the present moment is great, but daydreaming is a powerful tool. Mindful people love to visualize a positive outcome. It keeps them motivated, engaged, and productive. When it comes to complex and bigger projects, daydreaming has fascinating results.

"Imagination is more important than knowledge. For knowledge is limited to all we now know and understand, while imagination embraces the entire world, and all there ever will be to know and understand." – Albert Einstein.

280. Mindful people pause to reflect.

"Whenever you find yourself on the side of the majority, it is time to reform (or pause and reflect)." – Mark Twain.

Through the day, mindfulness people stop and reflect, they keep a journal or write their thoughts. Keep this tip in your back pocket because you can stop and review your thoughts and emotions from a distance. In the long run, mindfulness can help you to stop and consider your place in this world from time to time.

281. Practice mindfulness at work.

Believe it or not, you can train your mind to work better by practicing mindfulness. Through mindfulness, you gain the ability to focus your attention on your work. Mindfulness is the art of paying attention to what is going on in your life right here and now. You will learn how to be present at work; it improves your productivity and creativity, as well as leadership skills. As a bonus, you will experience better relationships with your colleagues.

282. Stress-free lives.

Mindfulness is a great antidote to the stresses of our modern lives. Mindfulness practice reduces your stress. Stress is hurting our health, so that modern man is constantly looking for effective ways to reduce or eliminate it. When you establish a mindful daily routine, you will be able to cope with stress effectively. It is not easy to achieve, but mindfulness emphasizes the importance of the journey, rather than the final results.

283. Mindful people nourish their bodies.

Eating mindfully is very important part of mindful living. When we are present, we can smell and taste the food in a completely different way; we are able to turn a normal meal into amazing experiences for all senses. In other words, mindful people are aware of nutrition and they try to eat healthier and better. Food should give us all-day energy. Food can influence our body and mind, so that you need to eat a well-balanced diet.

284. They follow their dreams.

From time to time, ask yourself the following question: Do I feel that I'm moving towards my dreams in life? You can write your answers down. This question can be a real wake-up call. If you don't pursue your dreams, perhaps you live a mediocre life, without excitement and passion. It's really sad.

This exercise will help you to create a better life by living in the present moment and following your dreams at the same time. If you have never really enjoyed the present moment, you can't follow your dreams and vice versa.

285. Mindful people express their feelings.

That may sound obtuse, but we need to express some strong feelings such as pain or anger occasionally. Being in touch with your feelings is one of the essentials of mindfulness. It's just about being open.

Mindfulness will make you a better person. When you practice mindfulness, you learn to express how you really feel. This practice will also help you to create an emotional balance.

286. Mindful people know when to be quiet.

"Nothing strengthens authority so much as silence." – Leonardo da Vinci.

Imagine this situation. You sip your morning coffee, and enjoy the space of being able to only think of stillness. Without a TV, the Internet, cell phone, and other distractions. This practice is a great way to savor your life more. Give it a try!

287. They are thankful.

According to many positive psychology studies, an attitude of gratitude is a powerful tool to develop mindfulness and increase your general well-being. It is well known that grateful people are less likely to be depressed and anxious. Like mindfulness, gratitude is a skill that you can learn.

Mindful people learn to be grateful for the present moment as much as they can. Give it a try!

288. A gratitude list.

Mindful people have learned this simple truth – If you want to live a better life, make your gratitude list. If you fancy being like that, take a piece of paper, take a deep breath, and start writing.

Our brain has evolved to focus on weaknesses and disadvantages rather than good things. When something goes wrong, we just forget about all the wonderful things that are happening right in front of our eyes. And of course, we easily take things for granted. A deep sense of gratitude is a common result of meditation and mindfulness practice.

289. They are recording things they're grateful for.

Here's an easy way to develop your sense of gratitude. Recording things is a great reminder that you can create on your journey of mindfulness. People can easily take things for granted. If you like writing, it would be a great activity to bring some more mindfulness into the practice. Happiness indeed.

290. Mindful people create constantly.

"The painter has the Universe in his mind and hands." – Leonardo da Vinci

Mindfulness practice develops and improves our creativity. It can get you into a state of heightened consciousness. Whether you write, paint, or compose a melody, you must be in the present moment. When it comes to creativity, you don't have to be an artist. You can dance, cook, or sing. Just be creative and let your imagination run wild!

291. A mindful person always seeks out new experiences.

That may sound obtuse, but life is an adventure. Mindfulness people enjoy both ordinary and extraordinary experiences. They live in the present moment and they love to be there. Life is full of pleasures and we often overlook them. Try slowing down and enjoying great things. Take time to stop and enjoy your life as a precious gift.

292. Make peace with imperfection.

"Being happy doesn't mean that everything is perfect. It means you've decided to look beyond the imperfections." – Unknown

By practicing mindfulness, your brain becomes linked with the now. And you realize that perfection doesn't exist. There is no such thing as the perfect moment or the perfect person. Every moment is a new beginning. Mindful people understand the rhetorical question: If not now, when?

293. Mindful people feel great.

Mindful people make the best of everything. And they feel great because of that. Mindful people are happy people; happy people shine like diamonds. If you are kind to someone else, that person is likely to feel good as well. In this way, you spread happiness to those around you.

294. Feel connected with others.

We are all interdependent on each other. Here are a few tips to become more connected with other people.

a. First and foremost, focus on how you can help.

b. Perform an act of kindness for others and watch the reactions.

c. Initiate meaningful conversations anytime you can.

d. Open your mind and make an effort to change your beliefs about the world and others.

295. Practice compassion.

Mindfulness definitely makes you more compassionate. Mindful people make it a daily practice. They practice forgiveness and acceptance as well, so that compassion becomes a part of their life. You can practice compassion meditation as well. Mindfulness and compassion go hand in hand.

"Love and compassion are necessities, not luxuries. Without them humanity cannot survive." – Dalai Lama.

MINDFULNESS AND AN ATTITUDE OF GRATITUDE

Mindfulness is the starting point for gratitude.

The present moment is full of wonders and happiness! By practicing mindfulness and cultivating an attitude of gratitude, you learn to enjoy positive life experiences and accept the negative ones. Gratitude has a powerful effect on our happiness.

"Gratitude is the best way to feel Inner-Peace and Happiness." – Maddy Malhotra.

296. Gratitude for a new day.

"With the new day comes new strength and new thoughts."
– Eleanor Roosevelt.

Every new sunrise is a chance to find new opportunities. It's a chance to be thankful for your life and everything you have. Your life is your reflection; whatever you send out, comes back to you, just like a mirror. If you are thankful for your life, life will give you more things to be grateful for. It is a natural law.

297. Create an abundance mentality.

The systematic cultivation of wakefulness is a path to an abundant life. When a person creates an abundance mentality, everything is going to change in their life. Abundance is not only about money ad material wealth. Mindful people go beyond this superficial attitude and realize that abundance is much more than material wealth. In this way, a person cultivates an attitude of gratitude, discovering the core ways of living an abundant and mindful life.

"Cultivate the habit of being grateful for every good thing that comes to you, and to give thanks continuously. And because all things have contributed to your advancement, you should include all things in your gratitude." – Ralph Waldo Emerson.

298. Develop an appreciation for the present moment.

This may sound obvious, but it seems that our appreciation for the present moment is probably the most powerful way to become more mindful. The present moment is all you have. Just be thankful for this blessing in your life. Here's a great exercise to feel more grateful right now. You can practice this exercise for any length of time. Schedule this exercise in your calendar and stick to your practice. Over time, you'll see positive outcomes.

Step 1: Take a deep breath and exhale; count up to ten. It will relax your nervous system, which makes it a perfect opportunity to change your mind-set.

Step 2: Now, you can practice loving-kindness meditation, which is a perfect way to cultivate a life purpose. You'll feel refreshed.

299. Keep a gratitude journal.

This is a great tip to become more thankful in your life. When you write down what you feel grateful for, you add purpose and meaning to your life. If you are interesting in writing, you can write inspiring stories about celebrating life. You can also share them by using social media and try to inspire other people to make a better life.

Since you can make any regular activity a mindful one, you have a lot of reasons to be happy and grateful every day.

300. Our predominant thoughts.

Most of the time, we have negative thoughts. We think of our problems, disappointments, things that do not go well, etc. Over time, your negative thoughts become your predominant thoughts. Predominant thoughts influence your behavior. To discover your predominant thoughts, you can respond to the following question: "What do you think about most of the time?" Do you think about your blessings, joy, happiness, health, good relationships, etc. Or you think of lack, stress, anxiety, anger, etc.

Stepping back from your thoughts, you develop and increase your awareness. Thus, you can develop an appreciation for all things and people you have in your life. You can use a practical exercise to become aware of your thoughts. Turn your attention inwards to thoughts; take a few deep breaths, and step back from your thoughts.

301. Make a list.

This is a secret to living a happy life. Think about all you have to appreciate. Your parents, your family, friends, your health, your job and money, and so on. Write it down and get back to your list every day if possible. We are thankful when we are aware of what we have rather than what we don't. It will boost our happiness and overall well-being.

302. Grateful people are happiest people in the world.

Mindful people are grateful people. Actually, mindfulness is the starting point for gratitude. You are simply aware of all the things that are going well in your life and this knowledge makes you happy.

Using mindfulness practice, you can develop gratitude while doing regular activities such as cooking, cleaning the house, doing laundry, and so on. For example, when cooking dinner for your family, think about them. Think how lucky you are because you have a family, food that you can cook, your hands to cook, your nose to smell your meals, and so on. This attitude will bring you an instant happiness. Give it a try!

303. Tell someone you love them.

If you feel frustrated, try to tell someone you love them today. Tell them how much you appreciate them. Gratitude will make your life better in so many ways. According to many studies, gratitude is among the most positive attitudes to cultivate in your life.

304. Meditation and gratitude list.

Meditation allows us to be in touch with where we are right now. Meditation with your gratitude list is a good exercise to practice your gratitude and expand your awareness. Try adding at least one more thing each day to your gratitude list. Happiness indeed.

305. A mindfulness exercise to practice gratitude.

Mindful attitude is the core of gratitude. Here's a simple mindfulness exercise to practice gratitude.

Give yourself 3 to 4 minutes, and come up with as many positive aspects in your life as possible. You can be grateful for a sunny day, for your pet or your car, and other little things; it doesn't matter, as long as you feel good. It is recommended to do this exercise every evening, before going to sleep. However, it's up to you.

306. There is nothing lacking.

"When you realize there is nothing lacking, the whole world belongs to you." – Lao Tzu.

Mindfulness allows you to see that you live an abundant life. Actually, mindfulness can help you to develop an abundance mentality. This world is abundant with many things, possibilities, great people, and so on. If you are able to enjoy the abundance you have in the present moment, you will be able to enjoy your life to the fullest.

307. Respect your body and mind.

One of the key elements of mindful life is respecting your body and your mind. Mindfulness and awareness of the present moment are one of the greatest ways to practice gratitude.

When you are present in the moment, you are thankful for your wonderful body and your powerful mind. You become grateful for so many things: your immune system, your sense of sight, sense of hearing, sense of taste, sense of smell, your speech, the ability to speak, your legs, hands, and so on. As we said before, you can supercharge your gratitude list every day.

308. You should be grateful for everything.

That may sound obtuse, but you should be grateful for everything, good or bad. You might think like this: However, I couldn't see how I would be able to feel grateful for the bad things in my life. This statement involves a profound paradox. When you are thankful for all things in your life, both good and bad, you send a message to the universe – I believe in the process. I am grateful. Thank you. I love you.

309. Gratitude boosts happiness.

"Gratitude is the best way to feel Inner-Peace and Happiness." – Maddy Malhotra. Gratitude is a quality of mind that enables us to enjoy our life with greater clarity. By practicing mindfulness and cultivating an attitude of gratitude, you learn to enjoy positive life experiences and accept the negative ones. Gratitude has a powerful effect on our happiness.

Through the day, stop to reflect, and enjoy the present moment. Remember – your gratitude is now, if you live in the present moment. The present moment is full of wonders and happiness!

310. Self-worth and self-esteem.

Self-worth is one of the greatest benefits of mindfulness. An attitude of gratitude helps you to improve self-esteem. By practicing mindfulness, you will be able to realize how much you have accomplished in your life. Accordingly, you will feel more confident. By cultivating the attitude of gratitude, you will be more in tune with your life.

311. Thankfulness and inner peace.

"Gratitude makes sense of our past, brings peace for today, and creates a vision for tomorrow." –Melody Beattie.

Be open to this practice and you can easily find that sense of peace in your life. When you are relaxed thanks to the mindfulness techniques, you will be able to embrace each and every experience, whether they bring positive or negative emotions. In that way, nothing can affect your inner peace. Afterwards, you are able to enjoy authentic happiness. What else could be more important than that?

312. Like attracts like.

The theory behind gratitude is the belief that energy attracts like energy. As Zig Ziglar noticed, "The more you express gratitude for what you have, the more likely you will have even more to express gratitude for."

You constantly radiate energy across the universe. Respond to the following question: "Do you radiate positive energy?" Human can only understand this through first-hand experience so keep trying.

313. Dear Mother Earth: Thank you!

Embrace nature to raise your consciousness. Spending some time outside can boost your energy levels, as well as brain function. Being in nature makes us feel at peace. Accordingly, we become more grateful for this planet, all living beings, and this wonderful life.

"Nature never hurries: atom by atom, little by little, she achieves her work. The lesson one learns from yachting or planting is the manners of Nature; patience with the delays of wind and sun, delays of the seasons, bad weather, excess or lack of water." – Ralph Waldo Emerson.

314. Choose to be grateful.

That may sound obvious, but when you decide to embrace gratitude, you begin to elevate levels of consciousness. When you truly think about it, you might begin to realize that you live on autopilot. People might focus on the bad things that happened in their life. It doesn't have to continue to be that way, because you can choose to be thankful, paying attention on the good things rather than bad one. Simply like that.

315. Thankfulness is now.

In the modern world, it's easy to become lost in different things instead of enjoying what's right in front of us. In the other words, there are so many reasons to not live in the moment. This is what thankfulness is all about – you're not worried about what could happen, or what might happen; you live right here and right now. And you appreciate your current situation. Being thankful for what you have here and now could make you a happier and better person.

316. The richness of a life of gratitude.

By focusing on gratitude, you are aware of what you're working on at this very moment. You have no reason to think about your lack, especially the lack of money. Many researchers have found that grateful people are more likely to get rich in the life. It's pretty logical. When we are 100% devoted to our life at this particular moment, we can focus on our job and making more money. We are not concerned about the future, we work, live and earn money right now. In the long run, we are confident, by doing what needs to be done. That's it!

317. How to become "a money magnet"?

As we said before, it was shown that gratitude might help you to get richer. This may sound paradoxical, but it has been proven that grateful people are less materialistic as well. When you are grateful for your life, for your breath, your family and other things that people often take for granted, you become "a money magnet". When you are thankful, you get more, and, by the same token, when you are ungrateful, you get less. Simply like that!

318. Gratitude for a good experience.

Here's a simple exercise. Look back on the past few days; what were you focusing on? Do you remember any great experience? Were you thinking about what could have gone wrong? Answers to these questions honestly.

If you spend most of your time thinking about good experiences and you are grateful for them, you are on a good path. Keep up the good work. Otherwise, if you spend most of your time thinking about bad experiences, you need a little bit more practice.

319. Allow yourself to "absorb" your experiences.

Here's a great idea that can help you to live in the moment and be thankful for your experiences. Do not switch from one thing to another too fast. Life is lived in the moment. Allow yourself to stop and reflect.

When it comes to a beautiful experience such as a hug, kiss, or a delicious meal, stop and "absorb" it; enjoy with all your senses. Do not think about the future (e.g. I'm going to pick up my kids from school). Turn it into the wonderful feeling that lasts as long as possible. In this way, you are able to be thankful for that. On the other hand, if you experienced some bad things, just be thankful for the lesson and go on. Simply like that!

320. A gratitude exercise that can change your life.

Actually, things will not always go your way. It's perfectly natural. There's no need to be frustrated. All you have to do is to learn to be grateful for whatever life may bring to you. Here's a great exercise to learn this lesson. Put things in perspective! Remember an unpleasant situation have happened to you recently. Do you feel some negative emotions regarding that situation?

Mindfulness can help you to understand that all negative emotions have something to show us. "What can I learn from this?" – this is a great question to get the best out of your situation. Ultimately, you'll be thankful and happy.

321. Gratitude and inspiration.

Appreciation and inspiration go hand in hand. We can absorb inspiration from every moment, so that "stay awake" and listen to your inner guidance. When you're grateful for the present moment, you are ready to follow your heart. At the present moment, you are able to focus on possibilities instead of the problems. Thus, you are thankful and productive. If you are struggling to find inspiration, you might not be in the present moment. Practice mindfulness using these techniques and things will sort themselves out. Who or what inspired you today?

"Don't wait for the perfect moment. Take the moment and make it perfect." – Unknown author.

322. Notes of appreciation.

"Gratitude is not only the greatest of virtues, but the parent of all the others." – Cicero.

Here is a great exercise to practice gratitude. Write a note of appreciation. You can write this note to yourself. It is a quite challenging, but practice makes you better. Here are good examples:

    a. I thank you for being my forever friend. I love you.

    b. You deserve to be happy. I love you.

    c. Thank you for caring about yourself; thank you for caring about others. I love you.

BRING MINDFULNESS INTO YOUR DAY

Bring inner peace into your daily life.

There are numerous challenges that will occur on your spiritual path. After regular practice of mindfulness meditation, we will be able to find our inner peace anywhere. Once you become connected with your true self, once you are fully present, you will be able to reap the benefits of mindfulness every single day.

323. You can get anything you want.

Mindfulness is one of the most important components of self-cultivated spirituality. As we said before, we should embrace the present moment because it's all we truly have. What we focus on can become our reality. When you live in the now, when you are happy and content right here and right now, you can get anything you want in your life.

Here's a simple exercise to become aware of your goals, desires, and your potential. What is your dream in life? Write it down, whatever it is. Don't think that you are too old or too young, don't think about your education, your origins, nation, or whatever it is. Just respond to the simple question – What is your dream in life?

324. Your life is a reflection of your habitual thinking.

There is an old proverb: As you sow, so shall you reap. Mindfulness is not a new-age nonsense. The origin of this practice is rooted in Buddhist philosophy more than two and a half thousand years. According to this philosophy, your life is a reflection of your habitual thinking. Your habits affect your spiritual life.

By practicing mindfulness, you will be able to understand this timeless concept and become open to wonderful possibilities. In the long run, you will gain a new perspective on your thoughts as well. In the course of time, mindfulness can help you to identify habits that don't serve your well-being. The more activities you do mindfully, the more possibilities you'll have to create better choices and better life.

325. Spread your wings!

Don't take anything for granted. Embrace the present moment and be thankful for your experiences, both positive and negative. Every experience brings you a great lesson. Mindfulness can help you to understand the purpose of your experience. You're exactly where you should be at this moment in your life. You live in this moment, right? You are not in your past. You are not in your future yet.

This is a great exercise that can help you to understand the power of the present moment and spirituality. Complete the following sentence "I'll be happy when…" One possible answer could be: "When I get a relationship." It means, you don't live in the present moment. You are dreaming about your possible future and you are not happy. Highly spiritual people will tell you: Be happy right here and now and your desires will manifest.

326. Mindfulness can change the structure of the human brain.

"How spiritual you are has nothing to do with what you believe but everything to do with your state of consciousness." – Eckhart Tolle.

Mindfulness can change our brain's capacity. A number of studies have shown that meditation and spirituality can change the structure of the human brain. This is pretty logical. When we are mindful of our moment-to-moment experiences, we are able to cultivate a variety of skills that can affect different parts of our brain. Clarify what matters most in your life and commit to your aspirations. Through the day, stop to reflect. Ask yourself: Does this action serve my happiness? Write down all answers that come to your mind.

327. Putting wisdom into practice.

Mindfulness may contribute to physical, mental, and spiritual benefits. If you look at your own life, what can you see? Maybe, you should set clear intentions and step out of your comfort zone. When we have to deal with an awkward situation and we're afraid doing something, it's time to step out of our comfort zone.

Here are some examples: If you have a fear of public speaking, you should give a speech. If you have a fear of the dentist, you should go to the dentist. Easier said than done, but mindfulness might help you to overcome these obstacles and live your life to the fullest.

You can apply this concept to any area of your life. Face your fears and continue whatever you were doing with a mindful attention.

"Do one thing every day that scares you." – Eleanor Roosevelt.

328. Using mini meditations.

Mini meditations are perfect for busy people and they are simple to follow. Mini mindfulness meditation lasts three minutes and you can do this anywhere. Here's how it goes:

Step 1: Sit on a chair in a comfortable upright balanced position. Close your eyes.

Step 2: Focus on your breath. Slowly and gently breathe in and breathe out.

Step 3: When you notice your thoughts wandering astray, gently guide your focus back to your breath. When you are ready, slowly open your eyes; you will feel refreshed.

329. A practice to help you to feel centered and grounded.

Step 1: Sit in a chair in an upright position and close your eyes. Your feet need to be firmly on the ground.

Step 2: Feel the physical sensation of your feet on the floor.

Step 3: Slowly and gently breathe in and breathe out. Each time you breathe out, allow your feet to feel more rooted to the earth.

Step 4: Slowly and gently open your eyes. It feels like coming home.

330. Practice breath awareness.

Breathing is like an anchor that grounds us in the present moment. Throughout the day, stop and pay attention to your breath. People take their breathing for granted, but it is our blessing that has a lot of benefits. Breathing helps release tension and allows us to live in the present moment. Conscious breathing is an easy exercise you can practice whenever you want. Here is an easy breathing exercise for you.

Step 1: Sit in a chair or lay down; find a comfortable position.

Step 2: Do 8 to 10 abdominal breaths. Inhale and exhale slowly and mindfully.

Step 3: Now imagine breathing into a tense area (for example your lower back). Exhale, and allow the tension to go out with the air. Repeat until you feel the tension disappear.

331. We have a freedom of choice.

The quality of your life depends on your choices. Fortunately, we have a freedom to choose our experiences every day. Mindfulness helps us develop better insight into possible realities of physical life. Once you start practicing mindful living throughout the day, you realize – Happiness is a choice! This is one of the biggest laws of nature.

When you need to make a decision during the day, no matter how small or insignificant it is, try your best to respond to the following question: "Is this decision right for me, as well as for all those involved in it?" Remember – You have more than one option, so that follow your heart and make your decisions mindfully.

332. Take responsibility for your life.

"Parents can only give good advice or put them on the right paths, but the final forming of a person's character lies in their own hands." – Anne Frank.

In reality, we have an ability to make personal choices that are given to us by nature. Almost everything you have, you may use for both positive and negative purposes. You choose your life, your surroundings, your friends, your job, etc. You are responsible. Here are examples: The Internet, social media, teaching, etc. When dealing with a difficult situation, stop and ask yourself: "What can I take from this?" And repeat mindfully: "I am responsible!"

333. Everyday mindfulness challenge: Stop complaining!

As we said before, you have full responsibilities for your action and your thoughts. Keep that in mind next time you feel the urge to complain about other people or circumstances. For instance, if you feel wronged, stop and take a deep breath instead of complaining.

Step 1: Sit comfortably or take a short walk in nature. Use any of mindfulness techniques to calm your mind; do not think about anything else except the present moment.

Step 2: Keep breathing; slowly and gently exhale your negativity, and inhale the freshness and peace. Release anything that doesn't serve you such as anxiety, tension, and so on.

Step 3: When you notice mind-wandering, gently (without any judgment) bring your attention back to the breath. Take it easy, and try your best to feel relaxed and refreshed. This approach will provide you with a broader outlook. Good luck!

334. There will always be distractions.

Distractions are the biggest and most common obstacles to mindfulness. Because of that, we may want to give up so many times. Obviously, living in the present moment is not easy. Distractions come and go, but you should grow in your self-awareness. Actually, obstacles are there to help you realize who you truly are. Mindfulness involves self-observation and self-study, which would be useful in making good decisions and understanding our capabilities. This is easier said than done, but it is not impossible.

Here's a great tip that can help you with this issue. Remember – there's no such thing as "only one right way"; in fact, there are so many correct paths you can choose. When you notice an obstacle on your mindfulness journey, stop to reflect. There are two possible solutions. This might be a good lesson to help you grow and become stronger. Another solution is to consider another way.

335. Your goals and mindfulness.

Goals are great motivation in life, but you should be careful. When you are too attached to your goals, you start feeling negative and frustrated. You may ask yourself every day: When will it happen? When, when, when?! What if I'm just kidding myself? It's so frustrating.

This may sound paradoxical; you simply can't have goals in the present moment. Yes, but there is a big BUT. Mindfulness will help you to create a strong faith in your abilities. In the course of time, you will realize that opportunities are infinite! Thus, you have no reason to give up on your goals and you are able to overcome self-doubt.

336. Easy ways to stop doubting yourself.

People often tend to turn simple problems into complex ones. It happens because they doubt themselves. It is scientifically proven that people who often doubt themselves live on autopilot. They are inclined toward materialism, so that they don't understand the benefits of mindfulness, meditation, and spiritual practice in general.

Mindfulness strengthens your self-confidence and gives you the patience to wait for the right opportunity. To make the best of mindfulness practice, please stop comparing yourself to others. Your accomplishments are yours. It is ridiculous to compare your achievements to your colleagues' achievements. We are all different and everybody has his own path. Remember – mindfulness is not a competition, you're just on your own path.

337. Live is happier without blaming yourself.

Self-blame is one of the worst things you can do to yourself. It is an ugly truth for those who have a tendency to take everything too seriously and they are not aware that it is an emotional abuse. Mindfulness will help you to free yourself from this toxic form of an emotional manipulation. When something bad and unexpected happens to you, try this simple mindfulness exercise. Here's how it goes:

Step 1: Sit comfortably and take a few deep breaths.

Step 2: Imagine that you gently exhale all your negativity, and inhale peace and love. Release any emotion that doesn't serve you such as blaming, tension, etc.

Step 3: Now ask yourself: "What do I should learn from this?" Keep calm and listen to your answers in silence.

Enjoy this mindfulness exercise as long as you are comfortable.

Keep in mind that you don't have to get your answers in this point of meditation. They will come at the right time. Do not rush yourself and don't blame yourself because you "failed at meditation". Therefore, do not fall into the trap of blaming yourself again.

338. How to recharge your willpower?

In reality, whether you are enlightened or not, you can feel some lack of willpower occasionally. Spending too much time problem-solving or thinking negative thoughts can drain your willpower. Mindfulness practice is a great way to maintain and improve your willpower.

Your mindfulness practice of 10 to 20 minutes per day can help you succeed. This practice is extremely successful, especially if you have some big challenges like quitting smoking or losing weight.

A study conducted by an epidemiologist at Brown University has shown that mindful people may be better able to motivate themselves to stick with a diet or exercise program. They claim, "Mindful people are less likely to be obese and are more likely to believe they can change many of the important things in their life."

339. Mindfulness and comfort zone challenges.

"Life begins at the end of your comfort zone." – Neale Donald Walsch.

Staying in your comfort zone has become our way of life. Modern man fears, loss, pain, uncertainty, and other small or big things.

When you are ready to explore new things, it will move you to a more fulfilled and happier life. Mindful people that master the art of being in the present moment constantly push their boundaries and there are not afraid of changes. For example, if you are afraid to move to another city or even to a foreign country due to a new job opportunity, practice mindfulness regularly. Here are a few steps that will help you to get out of your comfort zone and let things come around:

    a. Bring awareness to your comfort zone. Use your favorite mindfulness technique to become aware of the present moment.

    b. Your comfort zone is actually a prison. Choose adventure, challenge, and happiness over comfort.

    c. Ask yourself this powerful question: "What will my life be like in 5 or 10 years if I stay within my comfort zone?

340. Master your mind.

"It is better to conquer yourself than to win a thousand battles. Then the victory is yours. It cannot be taken from you, not by angels or by demons, heaven or hell." – Buddha.

Here're two powerful questions to ask yourself today: Who's running your thoughts? Where did they come from?

Mankind has a powerful tool for creation – our mind. Unfortunately, it can be used for destruction as well. A number of studies have shown that mindfulness can change the structure of the human brain. Bring mindfulness into your day and you'll become aware of your inner critic soon. You will become aware of its destructive force that prevent you from being happy and content. You will also become aware of past programming that no longer serves you. Try to understand your thoughts in order to go beyond them, and use mindfulness to conquer your mind. You can do it!

341. Find your true home.

Just sit quietly in one place and watch your thoughts. After a while, you will be convinced that our true home is in the now. If you are still not happy, you are not at home. And you are not in the present moment. A continuous flow of thoughts makes our mind restless. If you feel restlessness, you are not at home, you are not in the now. Just quiet your racing thoughts, cultivate a thought-free wakefulness, and you'll find your true home.

342. How to remove the causes of restlessness?

As one of the most common symptoms of anxiety, restlessness is a complex problem. Luckily, mindfulness and meditation may help you to ease and even neutralize the symptoms of anxiety. Here is a simple exercise:

Step 1: Sit comfortably in one place and take a few mindful breaths.

Step 2: Try to study your thoughts; slowly and gently follow them as they come to your mind.

Repeat this exercise as many times as needed and you will realize that continuous flow of thoughts makes your mind restless. When you learn to control your thoughts, you can remove the cause of restlessness and anxiety in general. Your mind is like an ocean, and your thoughts are its waves. One day you will discover this truth – You can control your mind. What else could be more important than that?

343. Change is the only constant in human life.

"Change is inevitable. Change is constant." – Benjamin Disraeli.

If you have not already realized that change is the only constant in life, mindfulness can help you to embrace and love it. During your life, you can experience various changes – childhood, the adolescent phase, adulthood, and old age. Finally, we experience the death of our present body. Maybe you think that our life is a bundle of paradoxes. Actually, the end (death) of one phase of your life leads to the beginning (life) of another phase. Here is why we should embrace change:

a. You become more flexible and open-minded.

b. All the great things in your life are the results of some turbulent change.

c. Changes have an amazing impact on your personal growth.

d. Changes trigger progress in any area of your life.

e. It is a turning page; it is a new beginning; it is a chance to improve your life and step outside of your comfort zone.

344. Affirmations and mindfulness practice.

Affirmations, as words or phrases that can evoke a positive state of our mind, are not new-age nonsense. As a matter of fact, affirmations are rooted in science, in the form of Neuro-linguistic programming. As a powerful tool, it was founded by two neuro-scientists from the University of Santa Cruz, in the 1970's. After that, many successful people have been using the power of positive thought patterns.

Mindfulness and meditations may improve and establish your positive habits, which leads to success in all fields. Try to practice affirmations a few times a day and record your progress. Because we learn best from first hand experiences, you can practice affirmations along with mindfulness meditation. Good luck!

345. How to practice mindful affirmations?

As you probably already know, being in a meditative state is our nature. The goal of mindfulness is to allow your thoughts to come up naturally. However, at the very beginning, mindfulness meditation can be challenging.

Here are a few mindful affirmations you can use if you have any difficulties to maintain a meditative state. These affirmations are recommended by mindfulhub.com.

"With every meditation session, I become more patient and understanding."

"As my meditation practice develops, I am able to take action that benefits myself and others."

"After every meditation session, I am able to make better decisions."

"Through this sitting meditation a become more calm and at ease."

"My mindfulness practice helps me communicate in an authentic way."

346. Brain-boosting foods.

What you eat affects your mental and physical health. Eating habits significantly affect your mindfulness practice. For example, serotonin helps us feel happy. Dopamine improves our ability to get motivated. Then, L-theanine can help us feel concentrated and calm.

"Your body is precious. It is our vehicle for awakening. Treat it with care." – Buddha.

347. We are born to be happy and content.

Positive psychology researchers have shown that we are all born with a "happiness set point." In the other words, happiness is our natural state of being. Everything in our life has its benefits and it has its downfalls; but if you cultivate mindfulness, gratitude and compassion, we can remain at peace no matter what is going on around us. Afterward, this is the goal of human life.

348. Stop judging things.

As we said before, we begin our mindfulness practice by watching our thoughts. Mindfulness is a great way to practice detachment from your thoughts and other things. In that way, you stop judging things and other people. As you bring more mindfulness into your life, you become more aware of this material world. This is the point where we stop judging and start living our lives fully. Happiness indeed!

349. A simple and short exercise.

This mindfulness exercise takes less than one minute, but brings a lot of benefits. This exercise is called "Two mindful bites". Actually, you should try mindful eating for the first two bites of your meal.

This exercise will help you to slow down your thoughts and enjoy your food with all your senses; once you achieve that, you need to just be in that state. It will also help you to control your eating and break bad eating habits. Good luck!

350. Consider aromatherapy.

This is a great advice, especially if you have any difficulties to maintain a meditative state. You can light a scented candle, which can help you to relax and enjoy your meditation to the fullest. In combination, mindfulness meditation and aromatherapy contribute to your psychological and physical wellbeing. Light candle, sit comfortably, and begin breathing. So relaxing.

351. Do not multitask.

Many of us believe that multitasking saves time. As a matter of fact, multitasking doesn't work. Human brain isn't designed to do several things at the same time. In general, it will take you longer to finish two or three projects when you're jumping back and forth; there is a great possibility to make mistakes as well.

You just need to stay focused on one task at a time. You can learn this skill by applying mindfulness throughout the day.

352. Give your brain a break.

Throughout the day, your brain must perform thousands of tasks. Give it a break every time you're able to do this.

Practice this exercise several times a day. Practice mindfulness in a short period of time rather than filling up every space in your schedule by reaching to check your phone or social media.

353. Bring inner peace into your daily life.

After regular practice of mindfulness meditation, you will be able to find your inner peace anywhere. Once you become connected with your true self, once you are fully present, you will be able to reap the benefits of mindfulness every single day.

There are numerous challenges that will occur on your spiritual path. Here are some of them. How to deal with negative people? How to find inner peace in the working environment? How to solve problems? Yes, it's very easy to apply inner peace and be fully aware of every situation as long as you are patient and you practice mindfulness. If you are able to control your mind, it will be free of reactive bad patterns. Accordingly, if you can control your mind, you will be able to control the situation.

354. The feeling of air on your skin.

This is a great exercise to motivate yourself in the midst of your hectic day.

Take a walk, preferably in nature, and mindfully pay attention to the feeling of air on your exposed skin for 1 minute. Practice this exercise every day and you will experience immense benefits. Remember – if you are fully present in right now, some great things are going to happen.

355. Mindfulness and healing.

Believe it or not, a lot of conditions in our body can be healed simply by practicing mindfulness throughout the day. Mindfulness may relieve stress and improve your physical abilities. There are many researches that have proven immense health benefits of mindfulness. Here's a practical exercise for those who are diagnosed with any disease. This exercise will also help you to deal with negative thought when they pop up. (Note: it isn't necessarily a cure-all, and medical treatment may be necessary).

Step 1: Sit comfortably and close your eyes.

Step 2: Take a few deep breaths, in your nose, out your mouth. Do not think about anything and keep breathing naturally.

Step 3: Focus on your health. Imagine you are completely healthy. Just focus on getting better and try to believe with all your heart.

When negative thoughts such as "I'll never get better", pop up, simply observe them instead of feeding into them.

356. I don't have time for this.

If you have such kind of excuse, it's time to begin a spiritual practice. The busier your life is, the more you crave the relaxation.

In reality, as you learn the mindfulness technique, you create more time for it. You can start with 1 minute a day. This one minute will be extended to 2 minutes, then to 3 minutes, and so on. Afterward, time is an illusion. It sounds weird, hopefully you will understand it by using mindfulness practice.

357. How will you know you're doing it right?

If you feel great and restful and if you have a sense of ease, that's it! Actually, you will know you are doing it right, you will know it intuitively. Don't worry about that, just focus on your practice and expect great outcome.

358. The "Do nothing" exercise.

This exercise will take only 3 minutes to experience amazing physical and mental benefits.

Step 1: Sit comfortably or lie down.

Step 2: Just notice where your mind goes. You can think about your dinner, your to-do lists, nothing, and everything.

This is your natural state. Your aim is to tolerate whatever your body and mind does, without the need to control something. Feel like you are just sitting here being yourself. You will feel perfectly at home. That's it.

359. Open up your senses.

Many studies have shown the benefits of mindfulness. As a matter of fact, you progressively have richer experiences of your body sensations and the world around you. Touch, smell, taste, and feel intensively, so that you begin to fine-tune your senses. Being conscious about what you're doing helps awaken your brain. You'll become open to receive pleasure in your life from all directions. Here are a few tricks that can help you.

a. Inhale strong scents such as essential oils or coffee beans. Breathe mindfully and don't think of anything else.

b. Try new foods and spices. Fresh ingredients are the best choice.

c. Go into nature and try focusing on what you see. Notice the lights, shadows, colors, etc. Then, sit comfortably and close your eyes. What are the sounds that come to your ear?

d. Take any object. How does it feel like? Feel its texture, weight, warmth or coldness.

360. Indulge in the things that you love.

Turn your ordinary routine into a spirit-renewing ritual. All you have to do is to perform your routine more slowly. Paying attention to your movement and your thoughts can center your mind. It's all about being mindful! For example, you can make your morning routine absolutely fantastic by doing something you love. Try to do anything that feeds your mind, even if it is something that just makes you feel like a child.

"Don't allow your life to become just a dead ritual. Let there be moments, unexplainable." – Osho.

361. Experience mindful parenting.

Parenthood is a spiritual path. First and foremost, mindful parenting is about seeing our children as they are. Actually, our children are spiritual beings coming to this world to grow and develop, just like you and me.

Mindfulness and spirituality are natural things for our children. Children are spiritual beings themselves, so that they can enrich our mindfulness. By looking at your child, you can see that he or she lives fully in the present moment. They know that this world is an interesting place full of adventures and wonders. As a parent, you will provide the most important part of a child's nurture and education, but don't forget to learn from children.

362. Magic of early morning.

You are more likely to maintain an inner calmness and balance of your mind if you enjoy waking up early in the morning. Early morning is the best time to devote some time for yourself, before all these demands and responsibilities.

Just sit for several minutes every day, in the morning, bringing awareness to your breath. It's a special space for just being. Focusing on the present moment will change your whole day. Throughout the day, when you notice imbalance, simply pause to reflect, and focus on mindful breathing.

363. Mindfulness at workplace.

Your work day is full of various distractions, so that it can make it difficult to stick to your mindfulness practice. Yes, it's difficult, but it is not impossible. Here are a few practical tips you can try the next time you start to feel overwhelmed at work.

a. A few times a day, focus on your breath; this is something you are able to control. It will help you to take back your power.

b. Mindfulness practice can help you to become less judgmental; thus, you will try to understand your colleagues instead of judging them automatically.

"In a world full of cynics, critics, and competitors, we get to choose instead to be cheerleaders for others." – Shelley Hendrix.

c. Mindfulness practice is a useful and reliable tool on your personal development journey, as well as in your work life.

364. An effective exercise for busy people.

"A good life is when you assume nothing, do more, need less, smile often, dream big, laugh a lot and realize how blessed you are for what you have." – Unknown author.

Take a deep breath and smile more often. Smiling makes you feel happier and less stressed. Mindfulness will train you to smile more. A few times a day, make a positive mental image; simply recall some happy memory, it will automatically boost your mood. Then, you can find a smile trigger (e.g. you can draw a little smiley face on a piece of paper and put it into your wallet). Remember – just be yourself!

365. Understanding the science of mindfulness.

Whichever way you look at it, mindfulness improves your life in so many ways. Mindfulness is an important part of human mental and physical health. It brings us the beauty of life.

Mindfulness practice reminds us of the blessings we may take for granted; freedom, health, peace, food and clean water, reliable electricity, a roof over your head, and so on.

Do not miss a very rare moment. You deserve a beautiful life!

Printed in Poland
by Amazon Fulfillment
Poland Sp. z o.o., Wrocław